FreeCAD 0.18

Learn by doing

Tutorial Books

For resource files contact us at
freecadtuts@gmail.com

Table of Contents

Introduction

Welcome to *FreeCAD 0.18 Learn by doing* book. This book is written to assist students, designers, and engineering professionals in designing 3D models. It covers the essential features and functionalities of FreeCAD using relevant tutorials and exercises.

Topics covered in this Book

- Chapter 1, "Getting Started with FreeCAD," gives an introduction to FreeCAD. The user interface and terminology are discussed in this chapter.

- Chapter 2, "Sketch Techniques," explores the sketching commands in FreeCAD. You will learn to create parametric sketches.

- Chapter 3, "Extrude and Revolve features," teaches you to create basic 3D geometry using the Extrude and Revolve commands.

- Chapter 4, "Placed Features," covers the features which can be created without using sketches.

- Chapter 5, "Patterned Geometry," explores the commands to create patterned and mirrored geometry.

- Chapter 6, "Sweep Features," covers the commands to create swept and helical features.

- Chapter 7, "Loft Features," covers the Loft command and its core features.

- Chapter 8, "Modifying Parts," explores the commands and techniques to modify the part geometry.

- Chapter 9, "Assemblies," helps you to create assemblies using the bottom-up and top-down design approaches.

- Chapter 10, "Drawings," covers how to create 2D drawings from 3D parts and assemblies.

Chapter 1: Getting Started with FreeCAD 0.18

Introduction to FreeCAD

FreeCAD is a cloud-based CAD application. It is a parametric and feature-based system that allows you to create 3D parts, assemblies, and 2D drawings. The design process in FreeCAD is shown below.

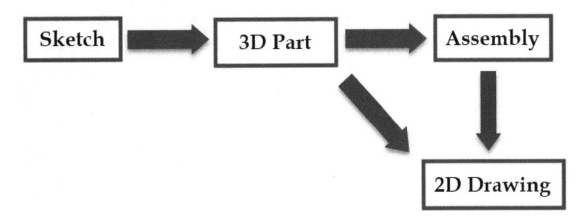

In FreeCAD, everything is controlled by parameters or constraints. For example, if you want to change the position of the hole shown in the figure, you need to change the constraint that controls its position.

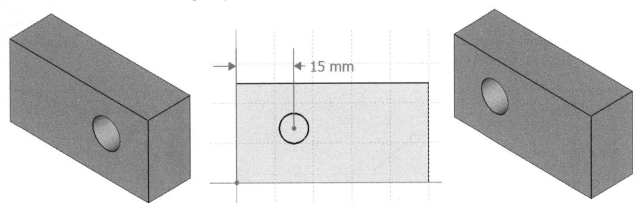

The parameters and constraints that you set up allow you to have control over the design intent. The design intent describes the way your 3D model will behave when you apply constraints to it. For example, if you want to position the hole at the center of the block, one way is to add constraints between the hole and the adjacent edges. However, when you change the size of the block, the hole will not be at the center.

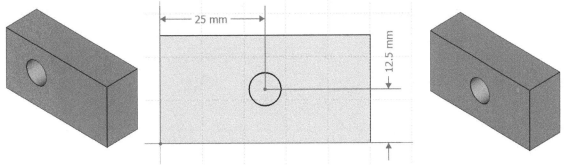

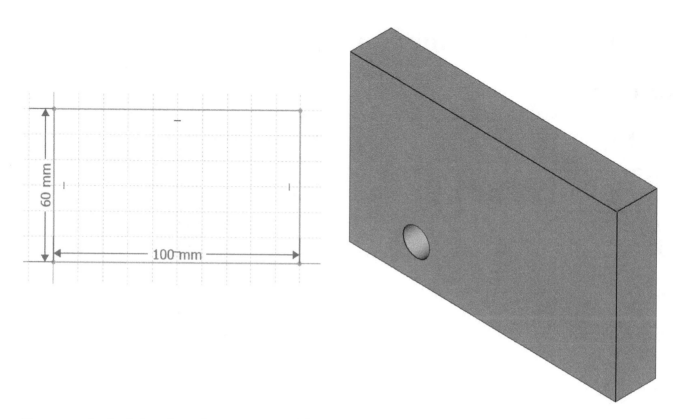

You can make the hole to be at the center, even if the size of the block changes. To do this, right click on the sketch used to create the hole and select **Edit sketch**. Next, delete the constraints and create a diagonal construction line. Apply the **Symmetrical** constraint between the hole centerpoint and the endpoints of the construction line. Next, click **Close** on the **Combo View** panel.

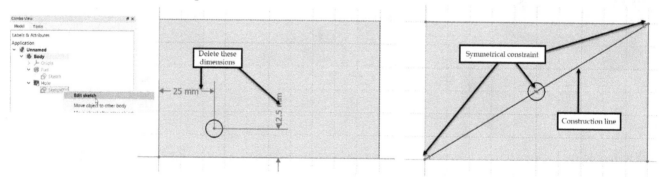

Now, even if you change the size of the block, the hole will always remain at the center.

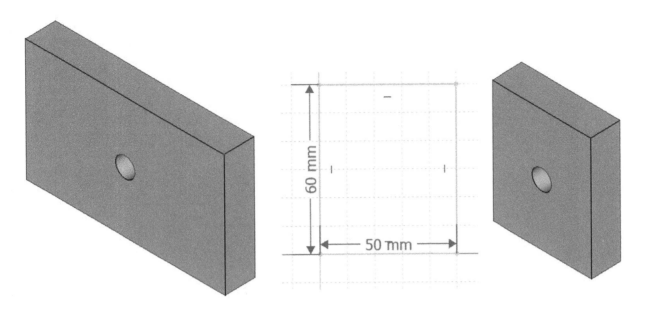

Starting FreeCAD

To start **FreeCAD**, click the **FreeCAD 0.18** icon on your Desktop (or) click **F > FreeCAD 0.18 > FreeCAD 0.18** on windows menu. On the **Start** page, click the **Documents** tab located at the top left corner, and then click **Create New**; a new design file will appear on the screen. You can change the working units of the file. To do this, click the **Edit > Preferences** on the menu bar. Next, click the **Units** tab and set the **User system** and click **OK**.

User Interface

The following image shows the **FreeCAD** application window.

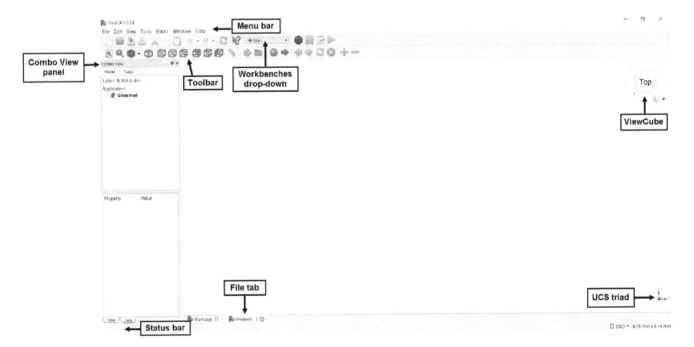

Graphics window

The Graphics window is the blank space located below the toolbars area. You can draw sketches and create 3D geometry in the Graphics window.

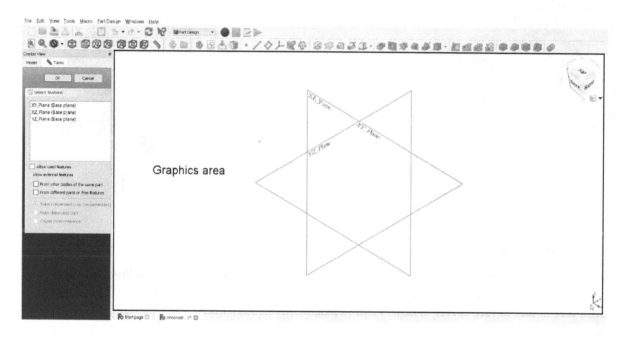

File Menu

The **File** menu appears when you click on the **File** option located at the top left corner of the window. The **File** menu has a list of open menus. You can see a list of recently opened documents under the **Recently Files** sub-menu.

Toolbars

A toolbar is a set of tools, which help you to perform various operations. Various toolbars available in the

FreeCAD are:

File Toolbar

This toolbar contains tools such as **New, Open, Save,** and so on.

View toolbar

This toolbar has the tools to modify the display and orientation of the model.

Workbench Toolbar

This toolbar allows you to change the workbench.

Macro

This toolbar has tools to create and execute macros.

View

This toolbar has tools to manipulate the view of the model.

Structure

It has tools to create or open part files.

Navigation

It has tools to open a website in FreeCAD.

Sketcher Toolbars

Sketcher

This toolbar has tools to start or exit a sketch.

Sketcher geometries
This toolbar has tools to create sketch elements.

Sketcher constraints
This toolbar has tools to apply constraints between sketch elements.

Sketcher B-spline tools
This toolbar has tools to create and edit B-splines.

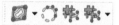

Sketcher Virtual Space
This toolbar helps you to hide or show constraints.

Sketch Tools
This toolbar has various selection tools and options that aid you in creating sketch elements very fast.

Part Design Toolbars

Part Design Helper
This toolbar has tools to create new bodies, datum points, axis, datum planes, and clones. You can also create or leave a sketch.

Part Design Modeling
This toolbar has commands to create solid features based on the sketch geometry.

Assembly 2 Toolbars

Assembly 2
This toolbar has tools to create components or insert existing components into an assembly. This toolbar also has tools to apply constraints between components.

Assembly 2 Shortcuts

This toolbar has tools to change the direction of the constraints, lock rotation, and insert multiple bolts into holes.

TechDraw Toolbars

TechDraw Views

This toolbar has tools to generate standard views of a 3D geometry.

TechDraw Clips

It has tools to add or remove clips to the drawing sheet.

TechDraw Pages

The tools on this toolbar help you to add a new page.

TechDraw Dimensions

The tools on this toolbar help you to add dimensions to the drawing views.

TechDraw File Access

This toolbar helps you to export the drawing page to the SVG format.

TechDraw Decoration

The tools on this toolbar help you to change the hatch patterns and insert images.

Some toolbars are not visible by default. To display a particular tab, click View > Toolbars on the menu bar. Next, select the toolbar from the sub-menu.

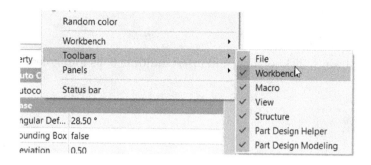

Menu

The menu is located on the top. It has various options (menu titles). When you click on a menu title, a drop-down appears. Select an option from this drop-down.

Status bar

The status bar is available below the graphics window. It shows the current status.

Preselected: Introduction.Sketch001.V_Axis (-39.251022,-15.000992,-70.322876)

Combo View panel

The Combo View panel located on the left side. It has two types: Model and Task.

Model tab

It contains the list of operations carried while constructing a part.

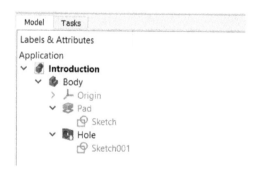

Tasks tab

When you execute any command in FreeCAD, the options related to it appear in the **Tasks** tab. The **Tasks** tab has various options. The following figure shows various components of this tab.

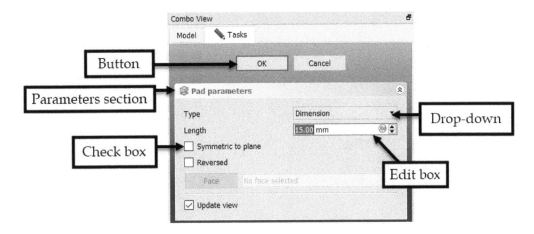

Mouse Functions

Various functions of the mouse buttons are:

Left Mouse button (MB1)

When you double-click the left mouse button (MB1) on an object, the parameters section related to the object appears in the Tasks tab. Now, you can edit the parameters of the objects.

Middle Mouse button (MB2)

Click this button to pan the view.

Right Mouse button (MB3)

Click this button to open the shortcut menu. The shortcut menu has some options to modify the display of the model.

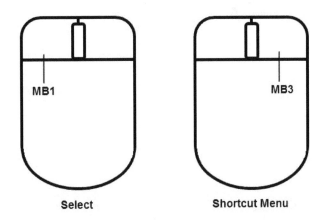

Edit Background

To change the background color of the window, click **Edit > Preferences** on the menu bar. On the **Preferences** dialog, click the **Display** option on the left side. Next, click the **Colors** tab and select **Background color > Simple color**. Click the color swatch next to the **Simple color** option. Select the white color from the **Select Color** dialog and click **OK**.

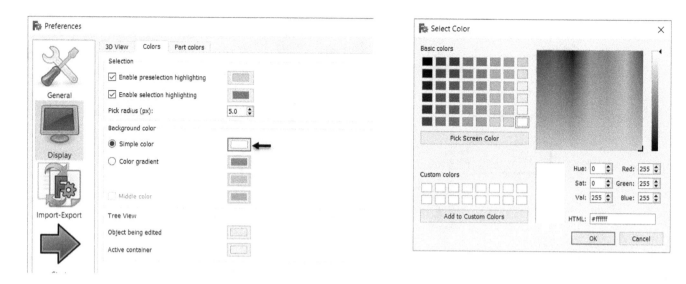

Click the **Sketcher** option on the left side of the Preferences dialog. Next, click the **Colors** tab and change the **Default edge color**, **Default vertex color**, **Edit edge color**, and **Cursor crosshair color** to black. Click **OK** to apply the changes.

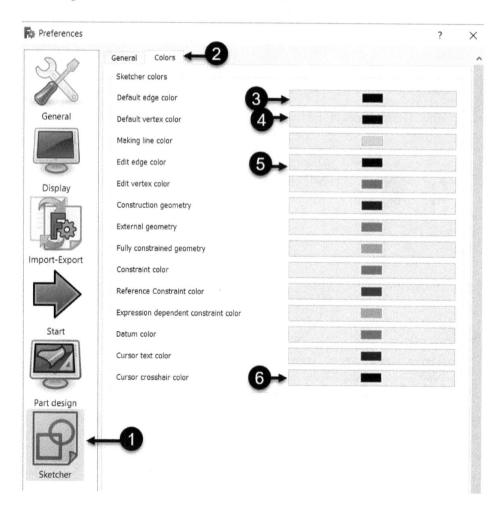

FreeCAD Help

FreeCAD offers you the help system that goes beyond basic command definition. You can access FreeCAD help by using any of the following methods:

- Press the **F1** key.
- Click **Help > Help** on the menu bar.

Questions

1. Explain how to hide or display toolbars.
2. What is the design intent?
3. Give one example of where you would establish a constraint between a part's features.
4. List any two procedures to access FreeCAD Help.
5. How to change the background color of the graphics window?
6. How is FreeCAD a parametric modeling application?

Chapter 2: Sketch Techniques

Tutorial 1 (Millimetres)

In this example, you will draw the sketch shown below.

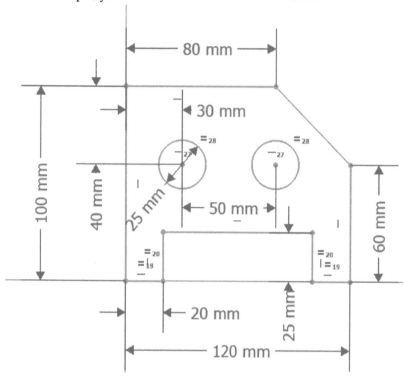

Starting a new part file

1. Click **FreeCAD** on the desktop to start.
2. On the Home page, click **Documents > Create New**; it creates a new document.
3. On the **Workbench** toolbar, select **Workbench** drop-down **> Part Design** (or) select **View > Workbench > Part Design** on the Menu bar.
4. Click **Edit > Preferences** on the Menu bar; the **Preferences** dialog appears on the screen.
5. Click **Units** tab and select **User system > Standard (mm/kg/s/degree)**.
6. Select **Number of decimals > 2** and click **OK** on the **Preferences** dialog.

Starting a sketch

1. To start a new sketch, click **Part Design Helper** toolbar **> Create a new sketch** (or) click **Part Design > Create sketch** on the Menu bar.
2. Select the **XZ_Plane** from the **Tasks** tab and click **OK**.
3. On the **Combo View** panel, click the **Tasks** tab and expand the **Edit Controls** section. Next, make sure that the **Show grid** checkbox is selected.
4. On the **Sketcher geometries** toolbar, click the **Polyline** icon (or) click **Sketch > Sketcher geometries > Create polyline**.
5. Click on the origin point to define the first point of the line.

6. Move the pointer horizontally toward the right and notice that the horizontal constraint symbol appears below the cursor.

7. Click to define the endpoint of the line.

8. Move the pointer vertically upward and notice the vertical constraint symbol below the cursor. Click to draw the vertical line.

9. Move the pointer horizontally toward the right and click.

10. Move the pointer vertically downward and click.

11. Move the pointer horizontally toward right up to a short distance and then click.

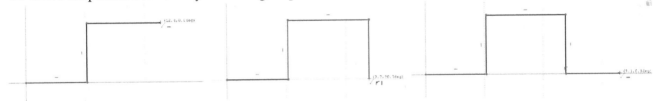

12. Move the pointer vertically upward and click.

13. Move the pointer in the top-left direction and click to create an inclined line.

14. Move the pointer horizontally towards left and click.

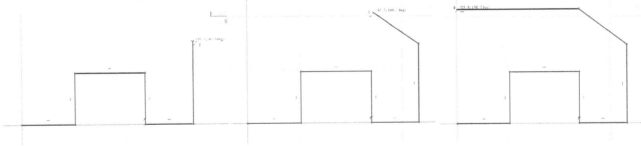

15. Move the pointer vertically downward and click on the origin point.

16. Press **Esc** twice or right-click twice to deactivate the **Polyline** tool.

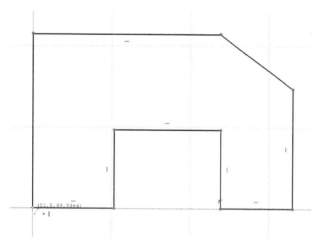

Adding Constraints

1. On the **Sketcher constraints** toolbar, click **Equal** ▦ . Next, select the two horizontal lines at the bottom; the selected lines become equal in length.

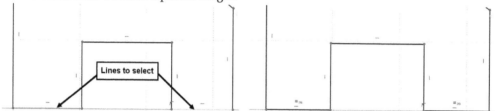

2. Select the small vertical lines; the selected lines are made equal in length.

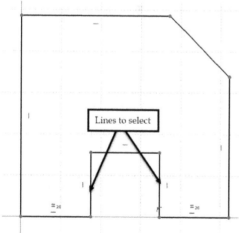

Adding Dimensions

1. On the **Sketcher constraints** toolbar, click the **Constrain horizontal distance** ⊢⊣ icon (or) click **Sketch > Sketcher constraints > Constrain horizontal distance** on the menu bar.
2. Select the bottom horizontal line of the rectangle.
3. Type-in **20** in the **Length** box of the **Insert Length** dialog and click the **OK** button.

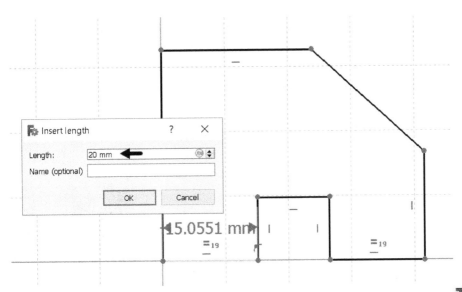

4. On the **Sketcher constraints** toolbar, click the **Constrain vertical distance** ⊥ icon (or) click **Sketch > Sketcher constraints > Constrain horizontal distance** on the menu bar.
5. Click on the small vertical line located at the left side. Move the mouse pointer towards the right and click to position the dimension.
6. Type-in **25** in the **Length** box of the **Insert Length** dialog and click the **OK** button.

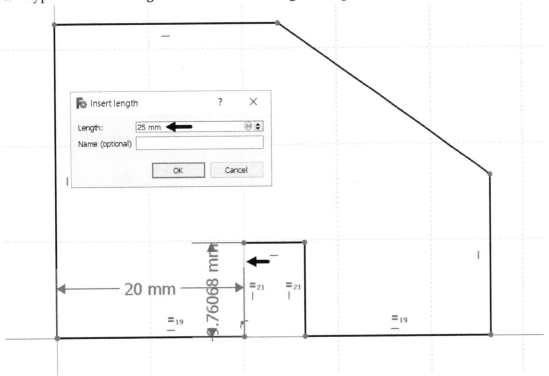

7. Create other distance constraints in the sequence, as shown below. Use the **Constrain horizontal distance** and **Constrain vertical distance** commands.

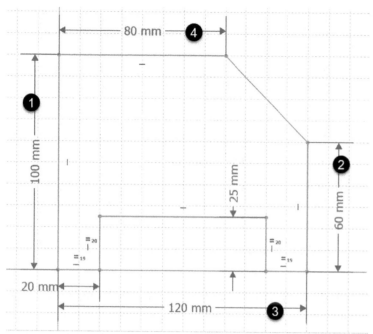

8. On the **Sketcher geometries** toolbar, click the **Create Circle** icon (or) click **Sketch > Sketcher geometries > Create Circle**.

9. Click inside the sketch region to define the center point of the circle. Move the mouse pointer and click to define the diameter. Likewise, create another circle.

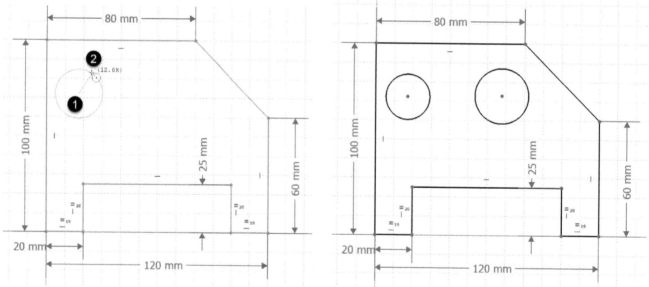

10. Press and hold CTRL key and click on the center points of the two circles. On the **Sketcher constraints** toolbar, click **Constrain horizontally** ▬; the centers of the circles are aligned horizontally.

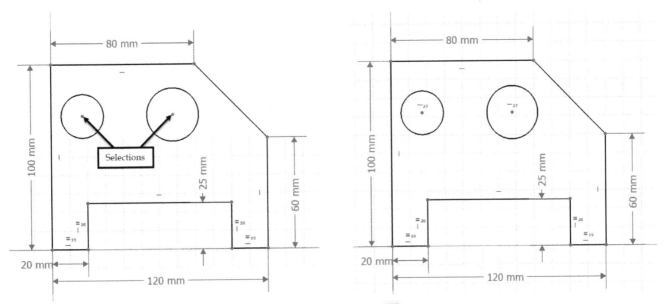

11. On the **Sketcher constraint** toolbar, click the **Constrain equal** ≡ icon. Next, click on the two circles; the diameters of the circles become equal.

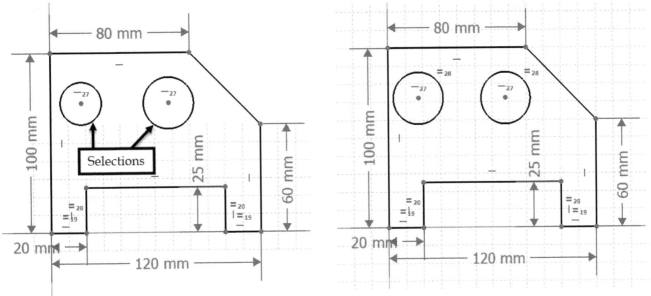

12. On the **Sketcher constraints** toolbar, Click **Constraint on arc or circle** drop-down > **Constrain diameter**.
13. Click on any one of the circles. Move the mouse pointer and click to position the dimension. Type **25** in the **Diameter** box and press Enter.

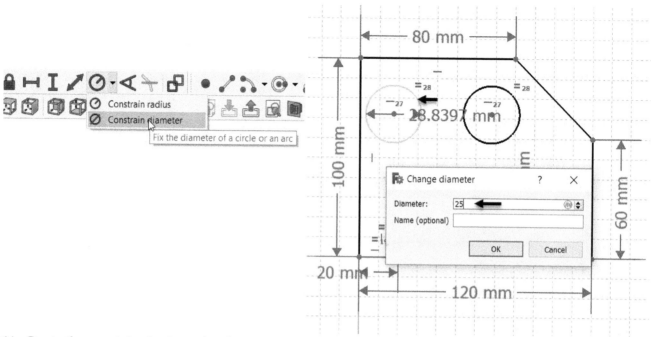

14. Create the remaining horizontal and vertical distance constraints between the circles and the adjacent lines, as shown below.

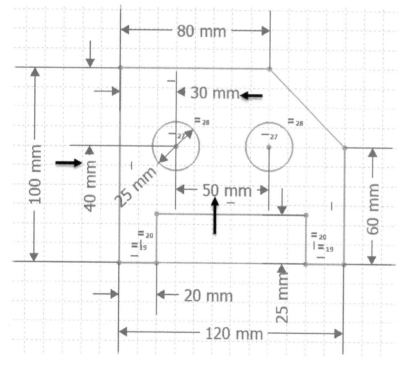

15. Click the **Close** button on the **Tasks** tab of the **Combo View** panel.
16. Click **File > Save** on the Menu bar. Next, browse to the required location on your computer and type **C2_example1** in the **File name** box. Click **Save**.
17. Close the file tab on the bottom left corner of the window.

Tutorial 2 (Inches)

In this example, you draw the sketch shown below.

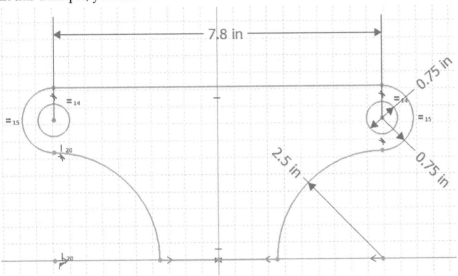

Creating a New document

1. Start FreeCAD
2. Click **Document > Create New** on the **Home** page.
3. Select the **Part Design** option from the **Workbenches** drop-down.

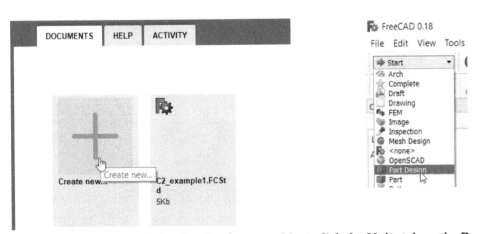

4. On the Menu bar, click **Edit > Preferences**. Next, click the **Units** tab on the **Preferences** dialog.
5. Select **User system > Imperial decimal**. Next, type **3** in the **Number of decimals** box, and then click **OK**.

Creating a Sketch

1. Click the **Create sketch** icon on the **Part Design Helper** toolbar.
2. Select the XZ Plane and click **OK** on the **Combo View** to start the sketch.
3. On the **Sketcher geometries** toolbar, click the **Create line** icon.

4. Click on the left side of the graphics window.
5. Move the pointer horizontally towards the right and click to draw a line.

6. Right-click to deactivate the **Create line** tool.
7. Click **Arcs drop-down > End points and rim point arc** on the **Sketcher geometries** toolbar and click on the endpoint of the line.
8. Move the pointer in the top-right direction, and then click to define the endpoint of the arc.
9. Move the pointer and click to define the radius of the arc.

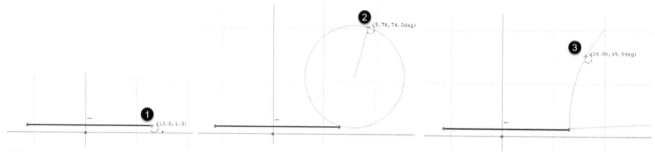

10. Click on the endpoint of the arc. Next, move the pointer upward and click to define the endpoint of the arc.
11. Move the pointer and click to define the radius of the arc.

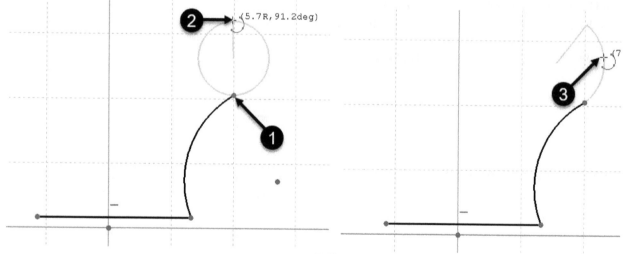

12. Activate the **Create line** tool (click the **Create line** icon on the **Sketcher geometries** Toolbar).
13. Select the endpoint of the arc.
14. Move the mouse pointer towards the left and click to create a horizontal line. Note that the length of the new line should be greater than that of the lower horizontal line.

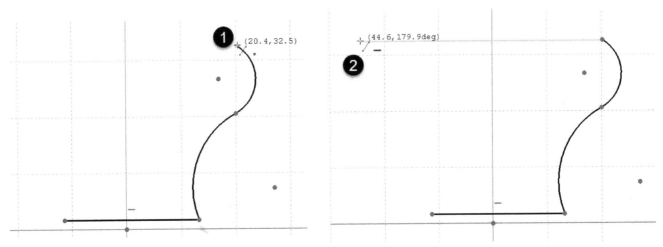

15. Press **Esc** to deactivate the **Create Line** tool.

16. Activate the **End points and rim point arc** tool and click on the endpoint of the line.

17. Move the pointer downwards and click. Next, move the pointer towards the left and click to define the radius of the arc.

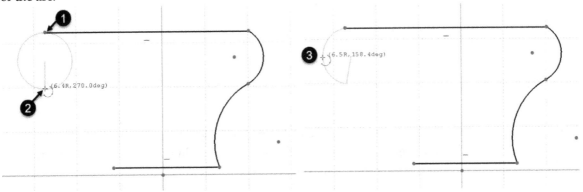

18. Click on the endpoint of the previous arc. Next, select the start point of the sketch.
19. Move the pointer and click to define the radius of the arc.

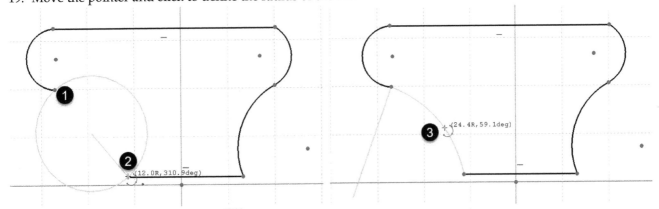

20. Click the **Constrain symmetrical** icon on the **Sketcher constraints** toolbar.
21. Select the left endpoint of the lower horizontal line, the right endpoint of the lower horizontal line, and the origin point. The endpoints of the horizontal line are made symmetric about the origin point.

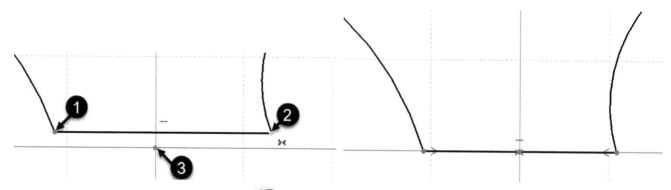

22. Click the **Constrain point onto object** ⌐ icon on the **Sketcher constraints** toolbar.
23. Select the center point of any one of the large arcs. Next, select the horizontal axis.

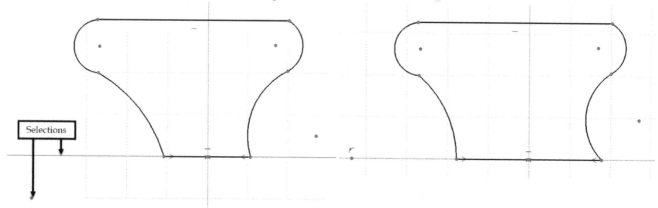

24. Click the **Constrain symmetrical** ⋈ icon on the **Sketcher constraints** toolbar.
25. Select the center point of the left large arc, the center point of the large right arc, and the origin point. The centerpoints of the arcs are made symmetric about the origin point.

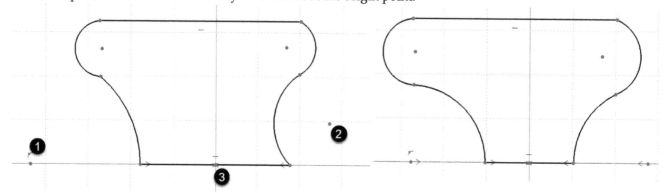

26. On the menu bar, click **Sketch > Sketcher geometries > Create Circle**.
27. Select the center point of any one of the small arcs. Next, move the pointer outward and click to create the circle.
28. Select the center point of another small arc, move the pointer outward, and then click.

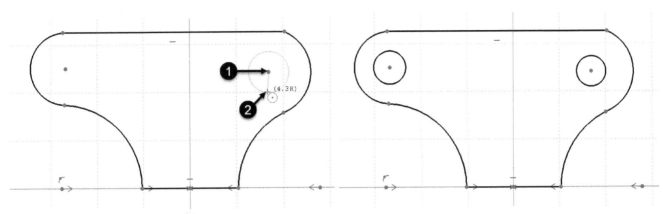

29. Click the **Constrain equal** ▬ icon on the **Sketcher constraints** toolbar. Next, select the two circles to make them equal in size.

30. Select the two small arcs to make them equal in radius.

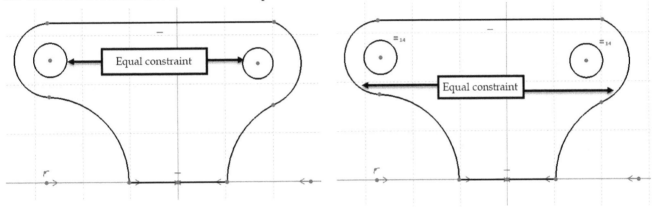

31. Click the **Constrain tangent** ↖ icon on the **Sketcher constraints** toolbar. Next, select the large and small arcs on the left side to make them tangent to each other.

32. Likewise, create the tangent constraints by selecting the other elements, as shown.

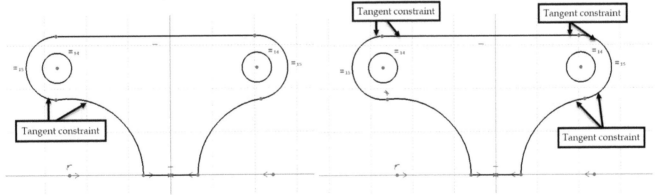

33. Press and hold the Ctrl key and select the centerpoint and endpoint of the left large arc.

34. Click the **Constrain vertically** ▮ icon on the **Sketcher constraints** toolbar; the selected points are aligned vertically.

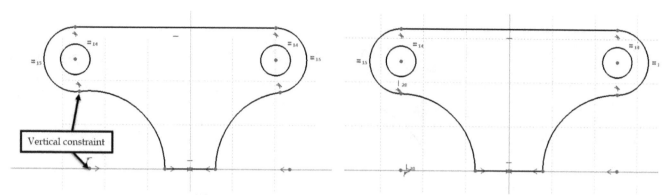

35. Click the **Constrain radius** ⊘ icon on the **Sketcher constraints** toolbar.
36. Select any one of the small arcs. Type **0.75** in the **Radius** box and click **OK**.

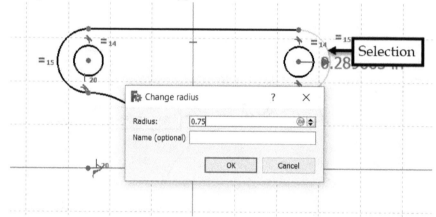

37. On the **Sketcher constraints** toolbar, click **Constrain radius > Constrain diameter**.
38. Select any one of the circles. Type 0.75 in the **Diameter** box and click **OK**.

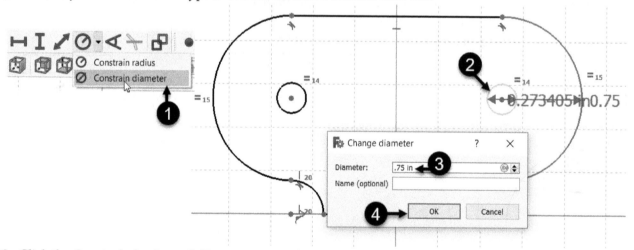

39. Click the **Constrain horizontal distance** icon on the **Sketcher constraints** toolbar.
40. Select the centerpoints of the two circles. Type 7.8 in the **Length** box and click **OK**.

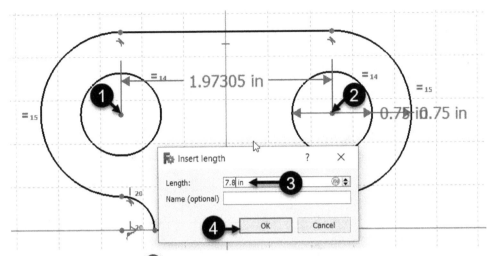

41. Click the **Constrain radius** ⊘ icon on the **Sketcher constraints** toolbar.
42. Select any one of the large arcs. Type **2.5** in the **Radius** box and click **OK**.

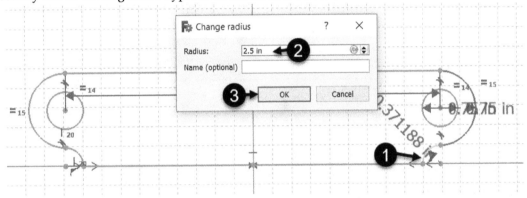

43. Click the **Close** button on the **Tasks** tab of the **Combo View** panel.
44. Click **File > Save** on the Menu bar. Next, browse to the required location on your computer and type **C2_example2** in the **File name** box. Click **Save**.
45. Close the file tab on the bottom left corner of the window.

Tutorial 3 (Millimetres)

In this example, you draw the sketch shown below.

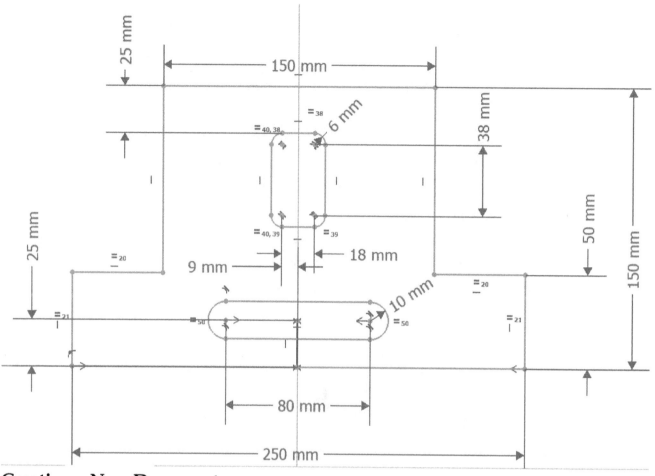

Creating a New Document

1. On the **Home** page, click **Documents > Create New**; it creates a new document.

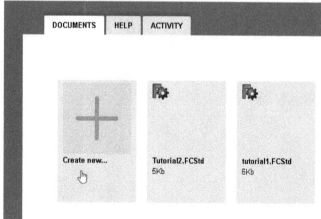

2. Click **Edit > Preferences** on the menu bar; the **Preferences** dialog appears on the screen.
3. Click **Units** tab on the dialog and select **User system > Standard(mm/kg/s/degree)**.
4. Select **Number of decimals > 2** and click **Apply**.
5. Click **OK** to close the **Preferences** dialog.

6. On the **Workbench** toolbar, select **Workbench** drop-down > **PartDesign** (or) select **View > Workbench > PartDesign** on the Menu bar.

Creating a Sketch

1. To start a new sketch, click **Create Sketch** tool on the **Part Design Helper** toolbar.
2. Select **XZ_Plane Select feature** section on the **Combo View** panel.
3. Click **OK** on the **Combo View** panel.

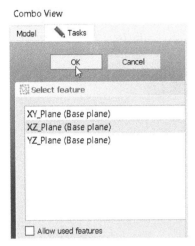

4. Activate the **Create line** tool (click the **Create line** icon on the **Sketcher geometries** toolbar).
5. Click on the origin point and move the pointer vertically up. Next, click to create a vertical line.

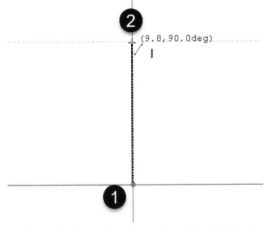

6. Press **Esc** to deactivate the **Create line** tool.
7. Select the vertical line and click the **Construction Mode** tool on the **Sketcher geometries** toolbar.

28

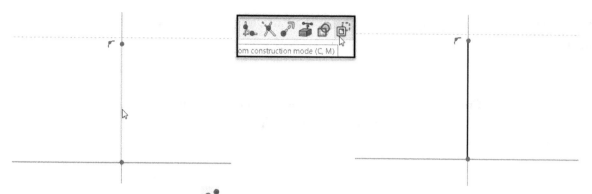

8. Activate the **Create polyline** tool and click the horizontal axis of the sketch on the left side of the construction line.

9. Move the mouse pointer vertically up and click to define the second point.

10. Move the pointer horizontally toward the right and click to create a horizontal line.

11. Move the pointer vertically up and click to create a vertical line.

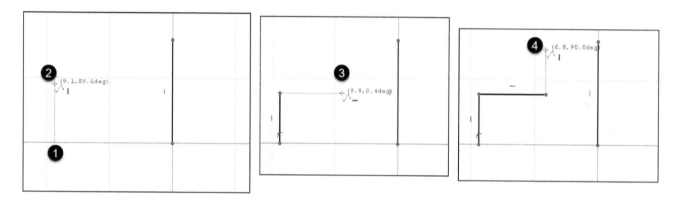

12. Press and hold the Ctrl key and select the lines and the construction line in the sequence given in the figure.

13. Click the **Symmetry** icon on the **Sketcher tools** toolbar (or) click **Sketch > Sketcher tools > Symmetry** on the menu bar; the lines are mirrored about the construction line.

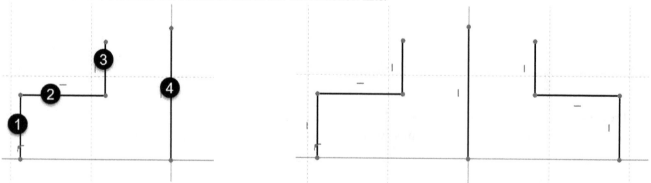

14. Activate the **Create line** tool (click the **Create line** icon on the **Sketcher geometries** toolbar

15. Select the endpoints of the lower vertical lines displayed on both sides of the construction line.

16. Select the endpoints of the upper vertical lines.

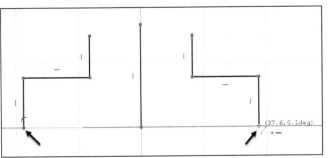 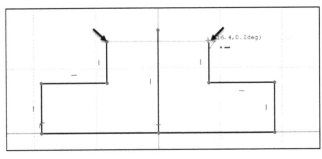

17. Press and hold the Ctrl key and select the endpoint of the lower-left vertical line, origin point, and endpoint of the lower right vertical line, as shown in the figure.

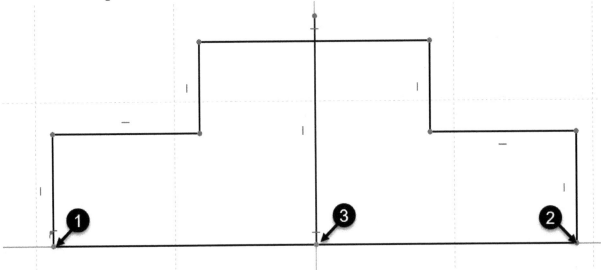

18. Click the **Constrain symmetrical** icon on the **Sketcher constraints** toolbar; the two endpoints are made symmetric about the origin point. Also, notice that the **Solver messages** section on the **Combo View** panel displays an error.

19. Click the **(click to select)** link in the Solver message. Next, scroll down in the **Constraints** section and notice that the **Constraint16** is highlighted.

20. Right click on the **Constraint16** and select **Delete**.

 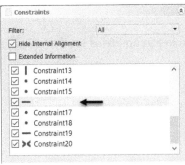 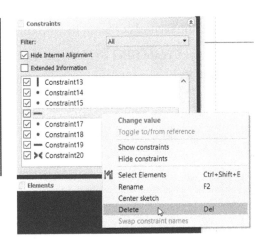

21. Click the **Constrain equal** icon on the **Sketcher constraints** toolbar

22. Select the two horizontal lines, as shown.
23. Select the two vertical lines to make them equal in length.

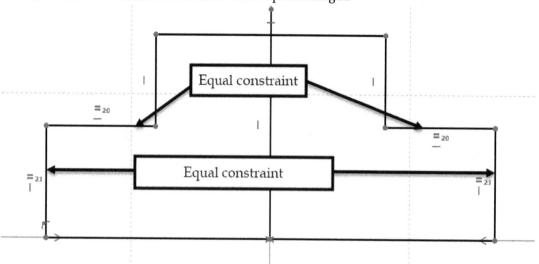

24. Create horizontal distance and vertical distance constraints, as shown.

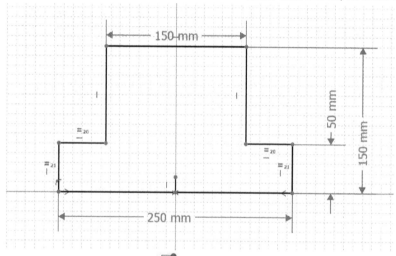

25. Click the **Create rectangle** icon on the **Sketcher geometries** toolbar.
26. Click on the left side to define the first corner of the rectangle. Next, move the cursor diagonally and click to define the second corner of the rectangle.
27. Click the **Create fillet** icon on the **Sketcher geometries** toolbar. Next, select the corner points of the rectangle.

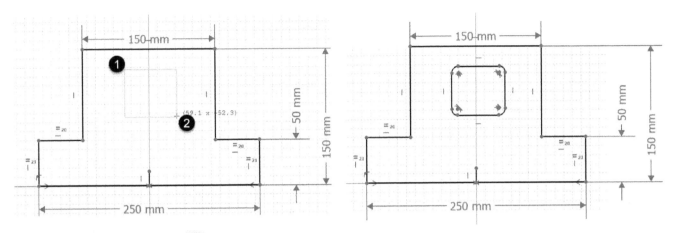

28. Click the **Constrain equal** ═ icon on the **Sketcher constraints** toolbar.
29. Select all the fillets of the rectangle in the clockwise direction. Next, select the first and last fillet to make them equal.
30. Click the **Constrain radius** ⊘ icon on the **Sketcher constraints** toolbar.
31. Select any one of the fillets. Type **6** in the **Radius** box and click **OK**.

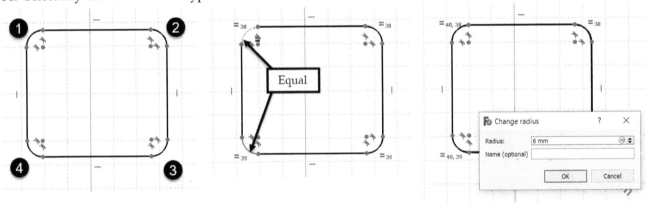

32. On the menu bar, click **Sketch > Sketcher constraints > Constrain horizontal distance**.
33. Select the centerpoints of the two lower fillets. Next, type 18 in the **Length** box and click **OK.**
34. On the menu bar, click **Sketch > Sketcher constraints > Constrain vertical distance**.
35. Select the centerpoints of the two right fillets. Next, type **38** in the **Length** box and click **OK**.

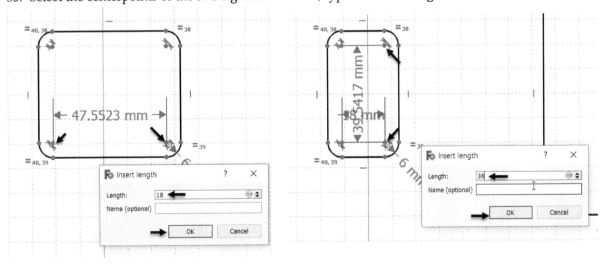

36. Click the **Constrain horizontal distance** ⊢⊣ icon on the **Sketcher constraints** toolbar.
37. Select the origin point of the sketch and the center point of the bottom-left fillet of the rectangle.
38. Type **9** in the **Length** box and click **OK**.

39. Click the **Constrain vertical distance** I icon on the **Sketcher constraints** toolbar.
40. Select the top-left corner of the outer loop. Next, select the top left corner of the rectangle.
41. Type 25 in the **Length** box and click **OK**.

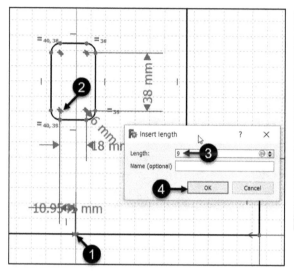 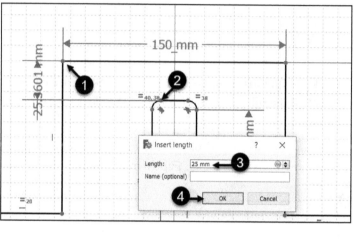

42. Click the **Create slot** ⊙ icon on the **Sketcher geometries** toolbar.
43. Specify the center point of the slot end on the left side of the sketch.
44. Move the pointer toward the top right and click to specify the other end of the slot.

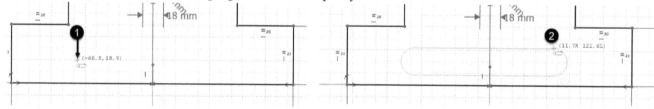

45. Select the endpoints of the slot and the top endpoint of the vertical construction line.

46. Click the **Constrain symmetrical** ⋈ icon on the **Sketcher constraints** toolbar; the two endpoints are made symmetric about the top endpoint of the vertical construction line.

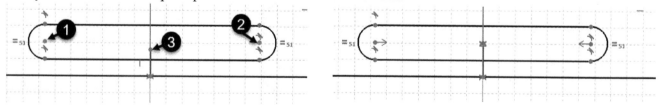

47. Add constraints to the slot and the vertical construction line, as shown.

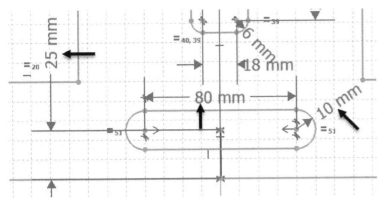

48. Click the **Close** button on the **Tasks** tab of the **Combo View** panel.
49. Click **File > Save** on the Menu bar. Next, browse to the required location on your computer and type **C2_example3** in the **File name** box. Click **Save**.
50. Close the file tab on the bottom left corner of the window.

Exercises

Exercise 1

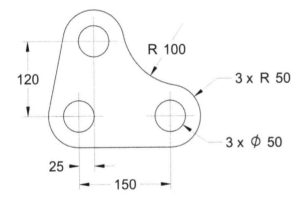

Exercise 2

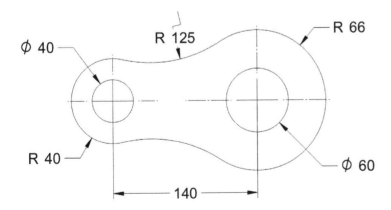

Exercise 3

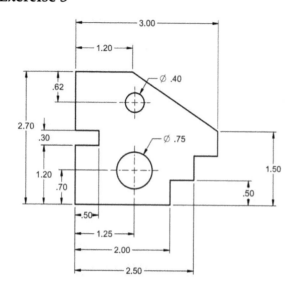

Chapter 3: Pad and Revolve Features

Tutorial 1 (Millimeters)

In this example, you create the part shown below.

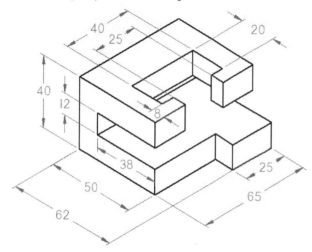

Creating a New Document

1. Click **FreeCAD** on the desktop to start.
2. On the Start page, click **Documents > Create New**; it creates a new document.
3. On the **Workbench** toolbar, select **Workbench** drop-down **> Part Design**.
4. Click **Edit > Preferences** on the **Menu** bar; the **Preferences** dialog appears on the screen.
5. Click **Units** tab and select **User system > Standard (mm/kg/s/degree)**.
6. Select **Number of decimals > 2** and click **OK** on the **Preferences** dialog.

Creating a Sketch

1. Click the **Create sketch** icon on the **Part Design Helper** toolbar, and then select the XZ Plane.
2. Click **OK** on the **Combo View** to start the sketch.
3. On the **Sketcher geometries** toolbar, click the **Create rectangle** icon.

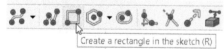

4. Click the origin point to define the first corner of the rectangle.
5. Move the pointer toward the top right and click to define the second corner — Press **Esc** to deactivate the tool.
6. On the **Sketcher Constraints** toolbar, click the **Constraint horizontal distance** icon. Next, select the horizontal line, type-in **50** in the **Length** box, and click **OK**.

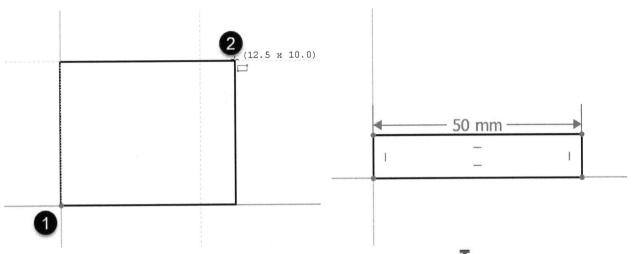

7. On the **Sketcher Constraints** toolbar, click the **Constraint vertical distance** $\mathbf{I}$ icon. Next, select the vertical line, type-in **40** in the **Length** box, and click **OK**.

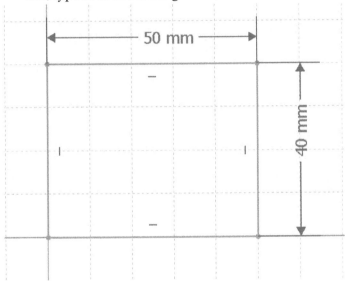

8. Click **Leave Sketch** on the **Part Design Helper** toolbar.

Creating a Pad Feature

1. Click the **Pad** icon on the **Part Design Modeling** toolbar.
2. Check the **Symmetric to plane** option on the **Pad parameters** panel.
3. Set the **Length** to **65** and click **OK** to create the pad feature.
4. Click the **Isometric** icon on the **View** toolbar.

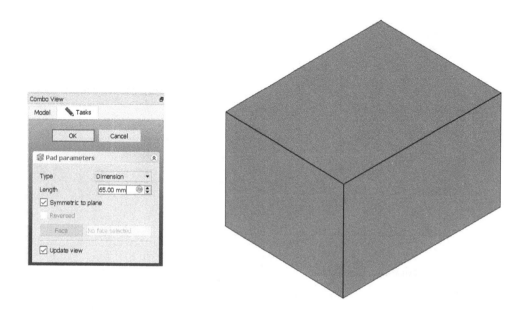

Creating an Extruded Cut Feature

1. Click on the front face of the part geometry. Next, click the **Create Sketch** icon on the **Part Design Helper** toolbar.

2. Click **OK** on the **Combo View** panel.

3. Click the **External geometry** icon on the **Sketcher geometries** toolbar. Click on the right edge of the model.

4. On the **Sketcher geometries** toolbar, click the **Create rectangle** icon.

5. Click on the right edge of the model, move the pointer toward left, and then click.

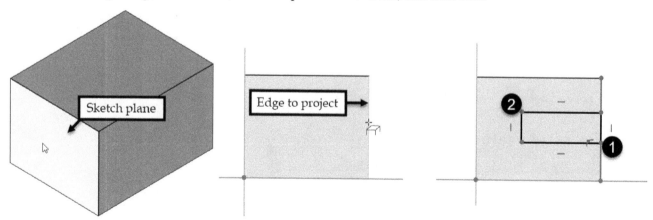

6. Activate the **Constraint horizontal distance** command and select the horizontal line of the rectangle. Next, type-in **38** in the **Length** box and click **OK** to add the dimension.

7. Click the **Constraint vertical distance** command and select the vertical line of the rectangle.

8. Type-in **12** in the **Length** box and then click **OK**. Make sure that the **Constraint vertical distance** is active.

9. Select the bottom right corner of the rectangle and the bottom endpoint of the projected edge, as shown.

10. Type-in **14** in the **Length** box and click **OK**.

11. Click **Leave Sketch** on the **Part Design Helper** toolbar.

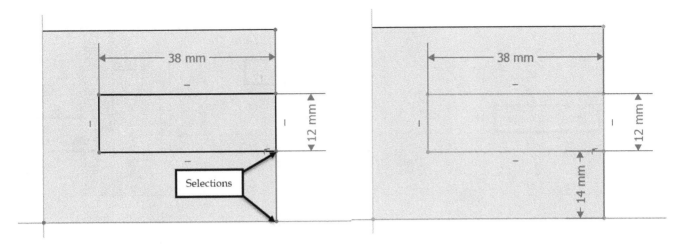

12. Click the Pocket [icon] icon on the **Part Design Modeling** toolbar.
13. On the **Combo View** dialog, under the **Pocket Parameters** section, select **Type > Through All**.
14. Click **OK** on the **Combo View** to create the cut throughout the part design.

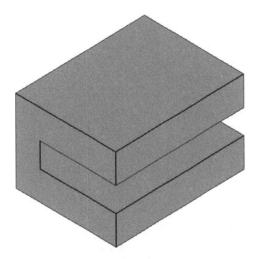

Extruding a sketch up to the Face next to the sketch plane

1. Click on the top face of the part design. Click the **Create Sketch** command on the **Part Design Helper** toolbar.

2. Click the **Set to top** [icon] icon on the **View** toolbar.

3. Click the **External Geometry** [icon] icon on the **Sketcher geometries** toolbar. Next, select the right vertical edge of the model; the selected edge is projected.

4. Activate the **Polyline** command (click the **Polyline** [icon] icon on the **Sketcher geometries** toolbar).
5. Create the sketch, as shown.
6. Select the inclined and click the **Constrain vertical** [icon] icon on the **Sketcher constraints** toolbar, as shown.

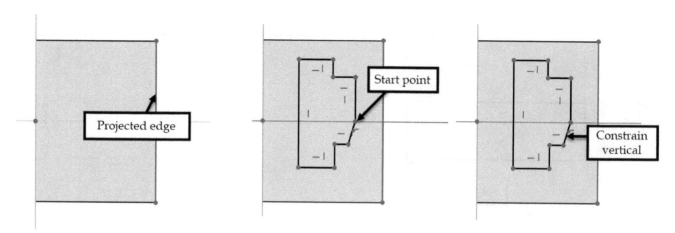

7. Click the **Constrain equal** ■ icon on the **Sketcher constraints** toolbar and select the horizontal lines, as shown. Next, select the vertical lines, as shown.

8. Click the **Constrain point onto an object** ⌐ icon on the **Sketcher constraints** toolbar and select the projected edge and the start point of the sketch. The selected point is made coincident to the projected edge.

9. Click the **Constrain equal** icon on the **Sketcher constraints** toolbar and select the vertical lines, as shown.

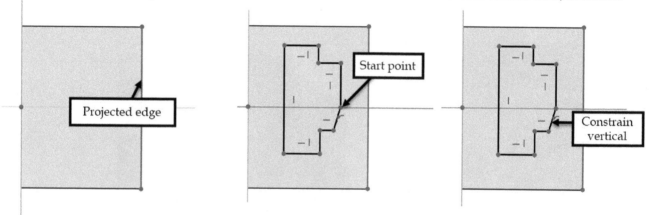

10. Click the **Constrain vertical distance** Ⅰ icon on the **Sketcher constraints** toolbar. Next, select the left vertical line. Type **40** in the **Length** box and click **OK**.

11. Select the endpoints of the right vertical line. Next, type 25 in the **Length** box, and then click **OK**.

12. Click the **Constrain horizontal distance** icon on the **Sketcher constraints** toolbar, and then select the left horizontal line. Next, type **20** in the **Length** box and click **OK**.

13. Select the right horizontal line and type **8** in the **Length** box, and then click **OK**.

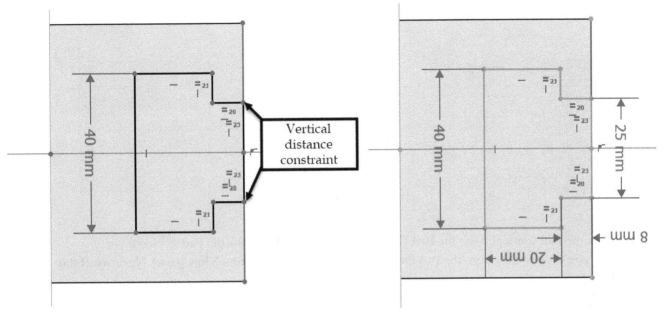

14. Click the **Close** button on the **Combo View** panel to close the sketch.

15. Activate the **Pocket** command (on the **Part Design Modeling** toolbar, click the **Pocket** icon)

16. On the **Pocket parameters** section, select **Type > To first**.

17. Click **OK** to remove the material up to the surface next to the sketch plane.

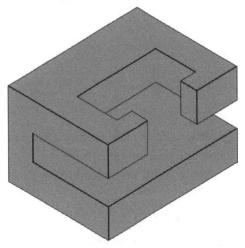

Extruding a sketch up to a selected face

1. Activate the **Create Sketch** command and select the XY plane. Next, click **OK** to start a sketch.

2. Draw a closed sketch and apply constraints to it, as shown.

3. On the **Sketcher constraints** toolbar, click **Constrain Coincident**. Next, select the corner point of the rectangle and the model, as shown.

4. Click the Close button on the **Combo View** panel to close the sketch.

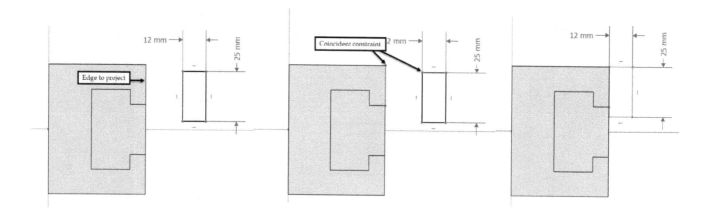

5.   Activate the **Pad** command (on the **Part Design Modeling** toolbar, click the **Pad** 🔲 icon)
6.   Select **Type > Up to face** from the **Pad Parameters** section on the **Combo View** panel. Next, select the horizontal face of the part geometry, as shown.
7.   Click **OK** on the **Pad parameters** section to complete the part.

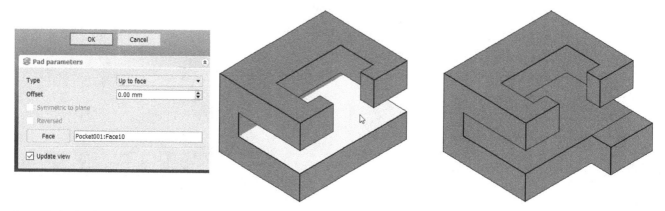

8.   Click the **Save** icon on the **File** toolbar located at the top-left corner of the window. Next, type C3_exampl1 in the **File name** box, and then click **Save**.
9.   Click **File > Close** on the menu bar to close the document.

Tutorial 2 (Inches)

In this example, you create the part shown below.

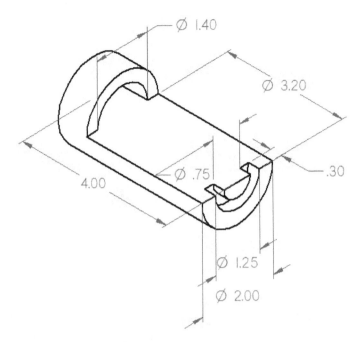

Creating a New document

1. Open a new FreeCAD file.
2. Click **Edit > Preferences** on the **Menu** bar; the **Preferences** dialog appears on the screen.
3. Click the **Units** tab on the **Preferences** dialog.
4. Select **User system > Imperial decimal** and type-in **3** in the **Number of decimals** box.
5. Click **OK** on the **Preferences** dialog.
6. Select the **Part Design** from the **Workbenches** drop-down.

Creating a Revolved Feature

1. Click the **Create sketch** icon on the **Part Design Helper** toolbar, and then select the XY_Plane.
2. Click **OK** on the **Combo View** panel.
3. On the **Sketcher geometries** toolbar, click the **Create rectangle** icon.
4. Click on the origin point to define the first corner of the rectangle.
5. Move the pointer toward the top right corner and click to define the second corner.

6. Click the **Constrain horizontal distance** 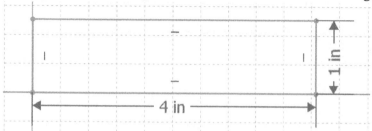 tool on the **Sketcher constraints** toolbar.
7. Select the bottom horizontal line. Next, type-in **4** in the **Length** box and click **OK** on the **Insert Length** dialog.
8. Click the **Constrain vertical distance** ⊥ tool on the **Sketcher constraints** toolbar. Next, select the vertical line.
9. Type-in **1** in the **Length** box and click **OK** on the **Insert Length** dialog.

10. Click **Leave Sketch** 📤 on the **Part Design Helper** toolbar. Next, click the **Isometric** 🔳 icon on the **View** toolbar.
11. Click the **Revolution** 🔩 icon on the **Part Design Modeling** toolbar.
12. Select **Axis > Horizontal Sketch Axis** from the **Revolution parameters** section on the **Combo View** panel.
13. Type-in **180** in the **Angle** box and check the **Reversed** option. Next, click **OK** on the **Combo View** panel to create the *Revolution* feature.

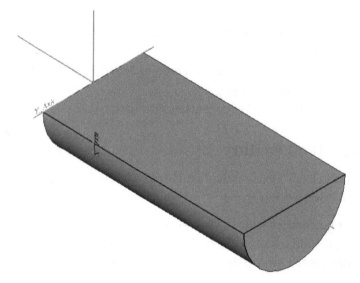

Creating a Groove feature

1. Select the top face of the part geometry and click the **Create Sketch** 🔲 tool on the **Part Design Helper** toolbar.
2. Draw a rectangle and apply the dimensional constraints to it, as shown.
3. Click the **External geometry** 🔩 icon on the **Sketcher geometries** toolbar and select the right vertical edge.
4. Click the **Constrain vertical distance** icon on the **Sketcher constraints** toolbar.
5. Select the top right corner of the rectangle and the top endpoint of the projected edge. Type **0.375** in the **Length** box and click **OK**.
6. Click the **Constrain point onto object** 🔩 icon on the **Sketcher constraints** toolbar and select the top right corner of the rectangle. Next, select the projected edge. Click the **Close** button on the **Combo View** panel.

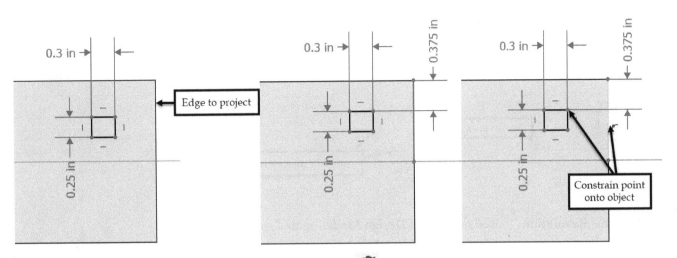

7. On the **Part Design Modeling** toolbar, click the **Groove** icon.
8. On the **Groove parameters** section, select **Axis > Horizontal sketch axis**. Next, type **180** in the **Angle** box and click **OK** to create the groove feature.

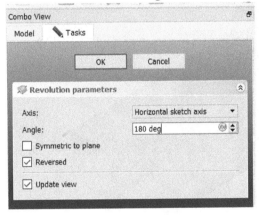

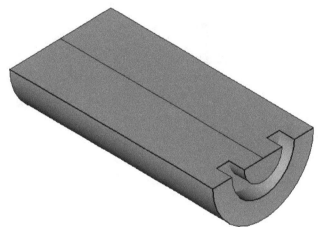

Adding a Revolution Feature to the Model

1. Select the top face of the part geometry and click the **Create Sketch** tool on the **Part Design Helper** toolbar.
2. Draw a rectangle and add dimensional constraints to it, as shown.
3. Click the **External geometry** icon on the **Sketcher geometries** toolbar and select the bottom horizontal edge.
4. Click the **Constrain coincident** icon on the **Sketcher constraints** toolbar. Next, select the bottom left corner point of the rectangle and the left endpoint of the projected edge.
5. Click the **Close** button on the **Combo View** panel.

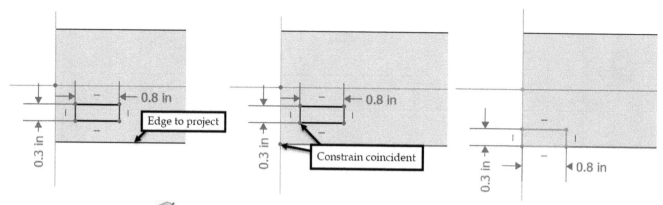

6. Click the **Revolution** icon on the **Part Design Modeling** toolbar.
7. On the **Revolution parameters** section, select **Axis > Horizontal sketch axis**.
8. Type 180 in the **Angle** box and click **OK**.

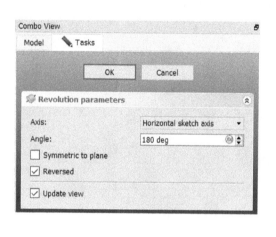

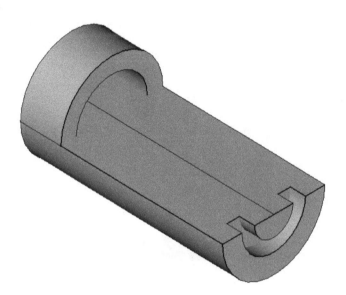

9. Click **File > Save** on the menu bar. Next, type **C3_example2** in the **File name** box, and then click **Save**.
10. Click **Close Tab** on the bottom left corner of the window.

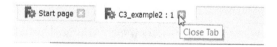

Exercises
Exercise 1

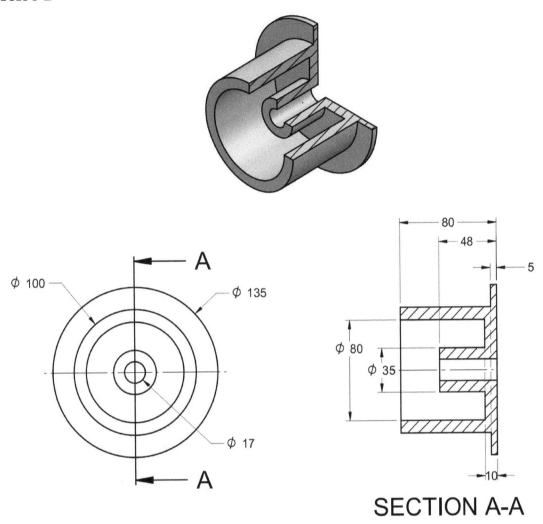

SECTION A-A

Exercise 2

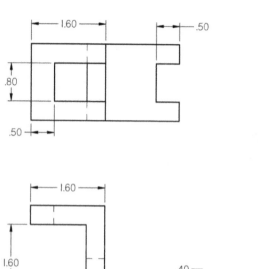

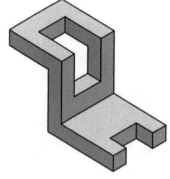

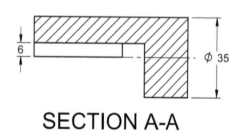

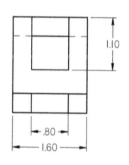

Exercise 3

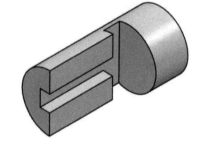

SECTION A-A

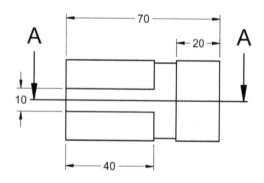

Chapter 4: Placed Features

Tutorial 1 (Millimetres)

In this example, you create the part shown below.

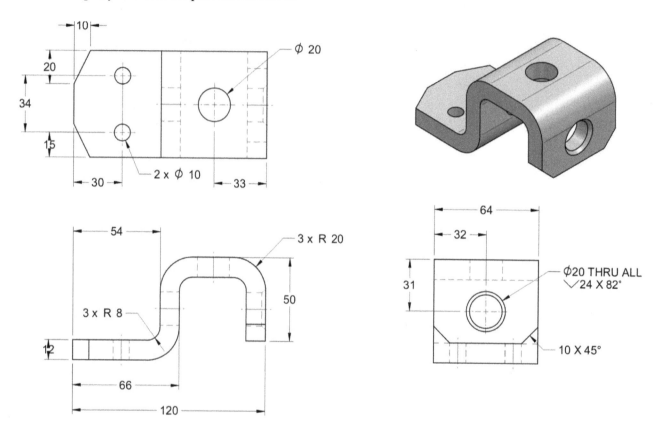

Creating a New document

1. Click **FreeCAD** on the desktop to start.
2. On the **Start** page, click **Documents > Create New**; a new document opens.
3. On the **Workbench** toolbar, select **Workbench** drop-down **> Part Design**.
4. Click **Edit > Preferences** on the **Menu** bar; the **Preferences** dialog appears on the screen.
5. Click **Units** tab and select **User system > Standard (mm/kg/s/degree)**.
6. Select **Number of decimals > 2** and click **OK** on the **Preferences** dialog.

Creating the Extruded Feature

1. Click **Create Sketch** command on the **Part Design Helper** toolbar and then select the **XZ** plane.
2. Click **OK** on the **Combo View** panel to start the sketch.
3. Click the **Create line** icon on the **Sketcher geometries** toolbar. Next, select the origin point of the sketch.
4. Move the pointer horizontally toward the right and click the horizontal line.
5. Click the **Constrain horizontal distance** icon on the **Sketcher constraints** toolbar. Next, select the horizontal line. Type **66** and click **OK**.

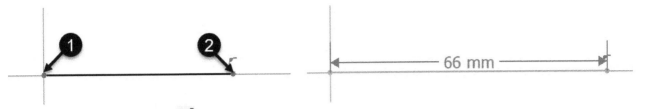

6. Click the **Create polyline** icon on the **Sketcher geometries** toolbar. Select the endpoint of the horizontal line.

7. Create a closed sketch, as shown below. Use the Constrain Coincident command and the endpoints, if they are not connected properly.

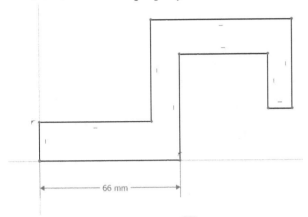

8. Click the **Constrain equal** icon on the **Sketcher constraints** toolbar. Next, select the small vertical and horizontal lines, as shown.

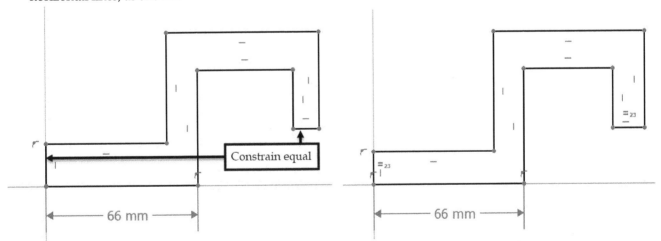

9. Click the **Constrain horizontal distance** icon on the **Sketcher constraints** toolbar. Next, select the points of the vertical lines, as shown. Type **120** and click **OK**.

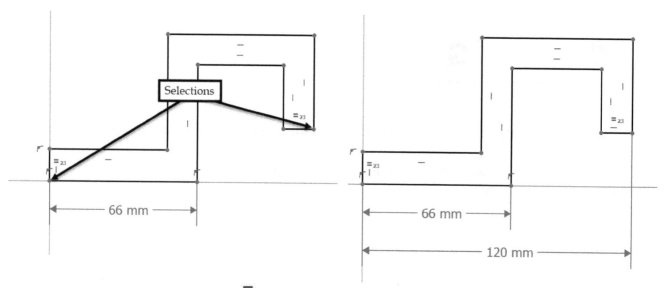

10. Click the **Constrain vertical distance** $\mathbf{I}$ icon on the **Sketcher constraints** toolbar. Select the corner point of the sketch, as shown. Type **62** and click **OK**.

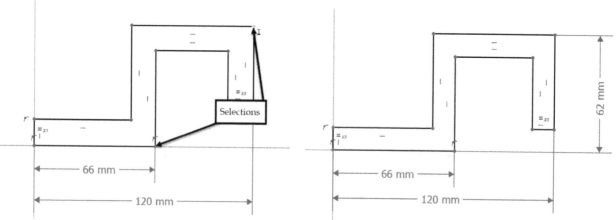

11. Add the remaining vertical and horizontal distance constraints, as shown.

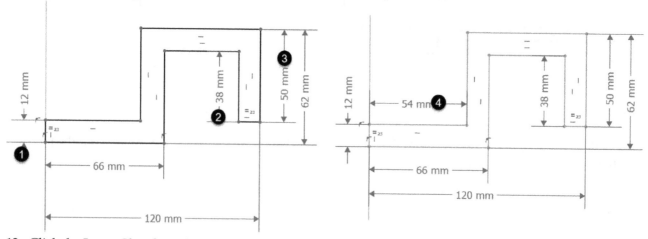

12. Click the **Leave Sketch** on the **Part Designer Helper** toolbar.

13. Click the **Pad** icon on the **Part Design Modeling** toolbar.

14. Type **64** in the **Length** box under the **Pad Parameters** section of the **Combo View** panel.

15. Select the **Symmetric to Plane** option and click **OK** to create the *Pad* feature.

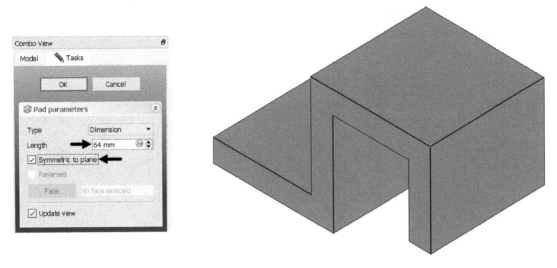

Creating the Hole Features

1. Select the right-side face of the model and click the **Create Sketch** icon on the **Part Design Helper** toolbar.

2. Click the **Set to right view** icon on the **View** toolbar.

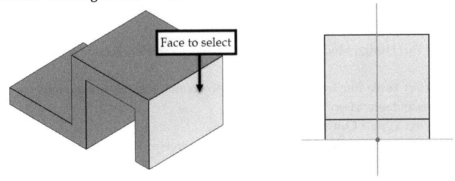

3. Click the **External geometry** icon on the **Sketcher geometries** toolbar.

4. Select the right vertical edge and the upper horizontal edge of the model, as shown.

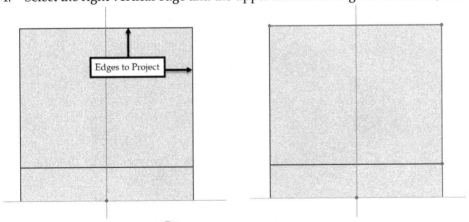

5. Click the **Create circle** icon on the **Sketcher geometries** toolbar. Next, select the vertical axis of the sketch to define the center point. Move the pointer outward and click to create a circle.

6. Click the **Constrain horizontal distance** 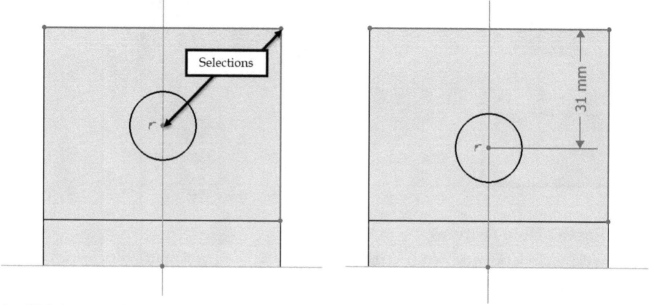 icon on the **Sketcher constraints** toolbar. Next, select the center point of the circle and the top right corner.

7. Type-in **31** in the **Length** box on the **Insert Length** dialog. Click **OK**.

8. Click the **Leave Sketch** icon on the **Part Design Helper** toolbar.

9. Click the **Hole** icon on the **Part Design Modeling** toolbar; the **Hole parameters** section appears on the **Combo View** panel.

10. On the **Combo View** panel, select **Threading and size >Profile > None** under the **Hole Parameters** section.

11. Type-in **21** in the **Diameter** box and select **Depth > Through All**.

12. Under the **Hole cut** section, select **Type > Countersink**.

13. Type-in **24** and **82** in the **Diameter** and **Countersink angle** boxes, respectively.

14. Click **OK** to create the *Hole* feature.

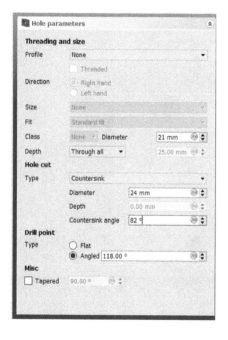

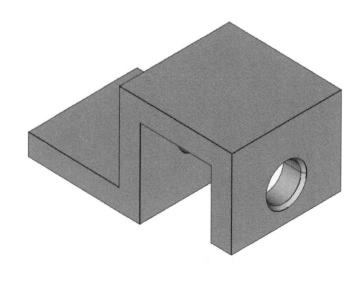

15. Select the top face and click the **Create Sketch** command on the **Part Design Helper** toolbar.
16. On the **Sketcher geometries** toolbar, click the **Create circle** icon and then select the horizontal axis. Move the pointer outward and click to create a circle.
17. Click the **External geometry** icon on the **Sketcher geometries** toolbar.
18. Select the left vertical edge and the upper horizontal edge of the model, as shown.
19. Click the **Constrain horizontal distance** icon on the **Sketcher constraints** toolbar. Next, select the center point of the circle and the bottom left corner.
20. Type-in **33** in the **Length** box on the **Insert Length** dialog. Click **OK**.

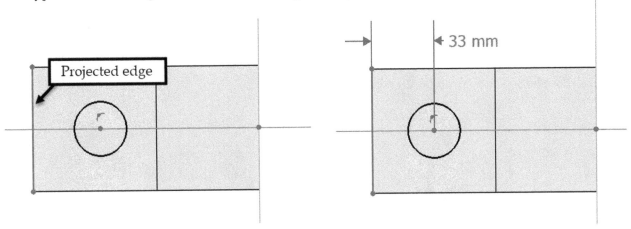

21. Click **Close** on the **Combo View** panel.
22. Click the **Hole** icon on the **Part Design Modeling** toolbar. Next, select **Profile > None** from the **Hole parameters** section.
23. Select **Depth > Through all**. Next, type-in 20 in the **Diameter** box.
24. Click **OK** to create the hole feature.

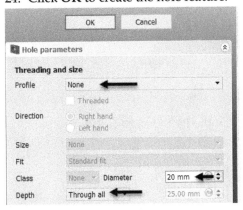

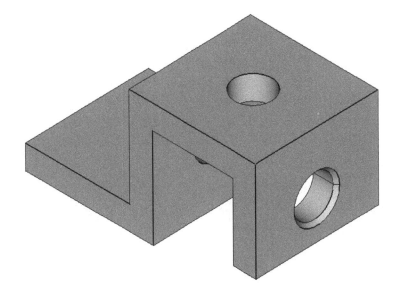

25. Select the lower top face of the model and click the **Create Sketch** icon on the **Part Design Helper** toolbar.
26. Click the **Create circle** icon on the **Sketcher geometries** toolbar and create two circles, as shown.

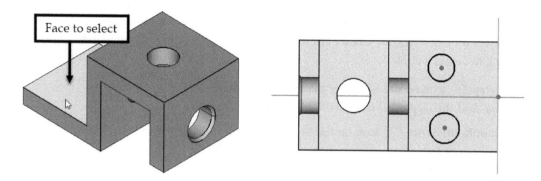

27. Create the dimensional constraints between the circles and the sketch origin.

28. Select the centerpoints of the two circles. Next, click the **Constrain vertical** ▌ icon on the **Sketcher constraints** toolbar to align them vertically.

29. Click the **Close** button on the **Combo View** panel.

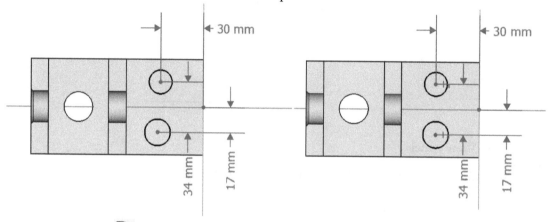

30. Click the **Hole** 🔲 icon on the **Part Design Modeling** toolbar. Next, select **Profile > None** from the **Hole parameters** section.

31. Select **Depth > Through all**. Next, type-in 10 in the **Diameter** box.

32. Click **OK** to create the hole feature.

Creating the Pocket features

1. Select the lower top face of the model and click the **Create Sketch** icon on the **Part Design Helper** toolbar.

2. Click the **Create Polyline** icon on the **Sketcher geometries** toolbar and create two triangles, as shown.

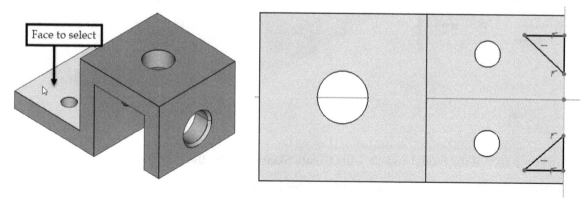

3. Click the **External geometry** icon on the **Sketcher geometries** toolbar.
4. Select the top and bottom horizontal edges of the model, as shown.
5. Click the **Constrain point onto object** icon on the **Sketcher constraints** toolbar. Next, select the corner point of the triangle and the projected edge, as shown; the point is constrained onto the projected edge.
6. Likewise, constrain the corner point of the other triangle to the remaining projected edge.
7. Add dimensional constraints to the triangles, as shown.

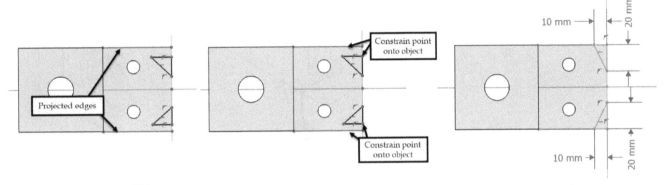

8. Click the **Pocket** icon on the **Part Design Modeling** toolbar. Next, select **Type > Through all** from the **Pocket parameters** section.
9. Click **OK** to create the pocket feature.

Creating Fillets and Chamfers

1. Press and hold the Ctrl key and select the edges of the model, as shown.
2. Click the **Fillet** icon on the **Part Design Modeling** toolbar.
3. Type **20** in the **Radius** box available on the **Fillet parameters** section of the **Combo View** panel. Click **OK** to create the fillets.

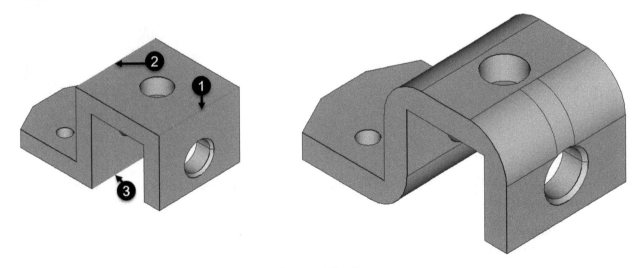

4. On the **View** toolbar, select **Draw style** drop-down > **Wireframe**.
5. Press and hold the Ctrl key and select the horizontal edges of the geometry, as shown.

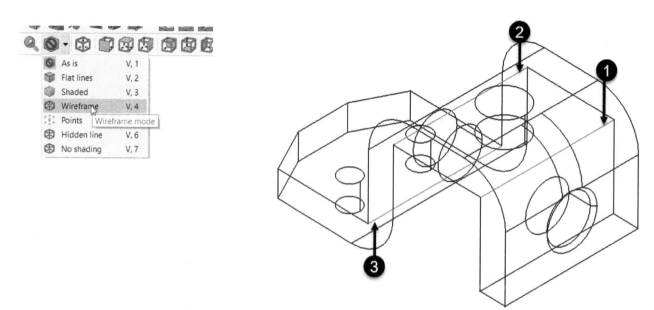

6. Click the **Fillet** icon on the **Part Design Modeling** toolbar. Type 8 in the **Radius** box of the **Fillet parameters** section, and click **OK**.
7. On the **View** toolbar, select **Draw style** drop-down > **Flat lines**.

8. Press and hold the middle and right mouse button, and then drag the cursor in the forward direction.
9. Press and hold the Ctrl key and select the edges of the model, as shown.

10. Click the **Chamfer** icon on the **Part Design Modeling** toolbar.
11. Type 10 in the **Size** box in the **Chamfer parameters** section. Next, click **OK** to chamfer the edges.
12. Click the **Save** icon on the **File** toolbar located at the top-left corner of the window. Next, type C4_example1 in the **File name** box, and then click **Save**.
13. Click **File > Close** on the menu bar to close the document.

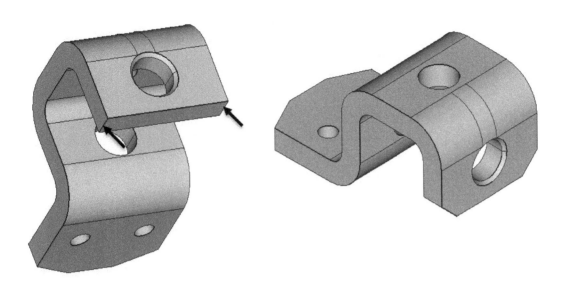

Tutorial 2 (Inches)

In this example, you create the part shown next.

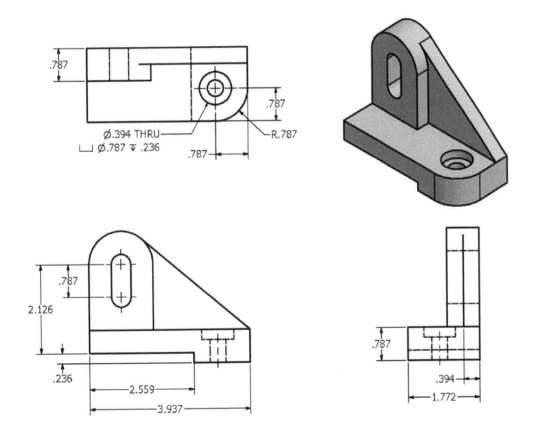

Creating a New document

1. Click **FreeCAD** on the desktop to start.

2. On the **Start** page, click **Documents > Create New**; it creates a new document.
3. On the **Workbench** toolbar, select **Workbench** drop-down **> Part Design**.
4. Click **Edit > Preferences** on the **Menu** bar; the **Preferences** dialog appears on the screen.
5. Click **Units** tab and select **User system > Imperial decimal**.
6. Select **Number of decimals > 3** and click **OK** on the **Preferences** dialog.

Creating the Extruded features

1. Click the **Create Sketch** icon on the **Part Design Helper** Toolbar and select the XY_plane. Next, click **OK**.
2. Click the **Create rectangle** icon on the **Sketcher geometries** toolbar and select the origin point of the sketch. Next, move the pointer toward the bottom right corner and click.
3. On the **Sketcher constraints** toolbar, click the **Constrain horizontal distance** ⊢ icon.
4. Select the lower horizontal line and move the pointer downward.
5. Type-in **3.937** in the **Length** box of the **Insert Length** dialog and click **OK**.
6. On the **Sketcher constraints** toolbar, click the **More** drop-down and click the **Constrain vertical distance** **I** icon.
7. Select the right vertical line and move the pointer towards the right.
8. Type-in **1.772** in the **Length** box on the **Insert Length** dialog and click **OK**.

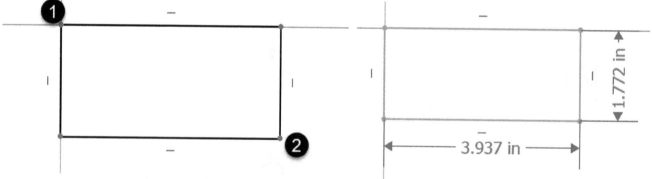

9. Click the **Close** button on the **Combo View** panel.

10. On the **Part Design Modeling** toolbar, click the **Pad** command.

11. On the **Pad parameters** section, select **Type > Dimension** and enter **0.787** in the **Length** box. Click **OK** to create the *Pad* feature.

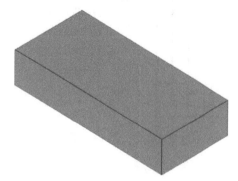

12. Activate the **Create Sketch** command and select the **XZ_plane** on the **Combo View** panel. Next, click **OK**.

13. Click the **Create rectangle** command on the **Sketcher geometries** toolbar and specify the first and second corners of the rectangle, as shown.

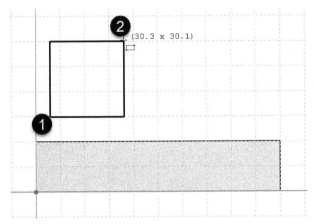

14. On the **Sketcher geometries** toolbar, click **Create an arc** drop-down > **End points and rim point** . Next, create an arc, as shown in the figure.

15. On the **Sketcher constraints** toolbar, click the **Constrain tangent** icon.

16. Select the arc and left vertical line to make the arc tangent to the line.

17. Likewise, select the arc and right vertical line to make the arc tangent to the line.

18. Select the horizontal line below the arc and press **Delete** key on the keyboard.

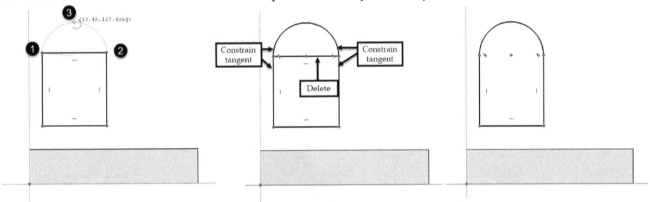

19. Click the **External geometry** command on the **Sketcher geometries** toolbar and select the horizontal line of the part geometry, as shown.

20. On the **Sketcher constraints** toolbar, click the **Constrain coincident** and select the endpoint of the sketch. Next, select the endpoint of the projected edge.

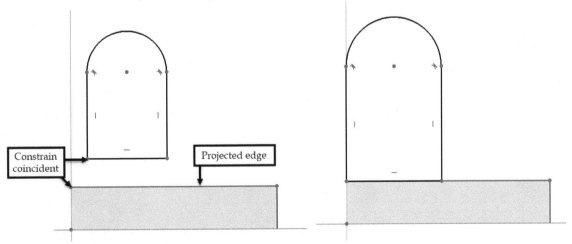

21. Click **Constrain vertical distance** on the **Sketcher constraints** toolbar. Next, select the left vertical line of the sketch.

22. Type-in **1.575** in the **Length** box on the **Insert Length** dialog. Click **OK**.

23. Click the **Constrain radius** ⊘ icon on the **Sketcher constraints** toolbar. Next, select the arc, type **0.787** in the **Radius** box, and then click **OK**.

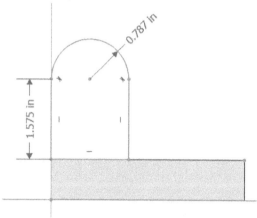

24. Click **Close** on the **Combo View** panel.

25. Activate the **Pad** 🗗 command select **Type > Dimension**. Next, enter 0.787 in the **Length** box. Click **OK** to complete the Pad feature.

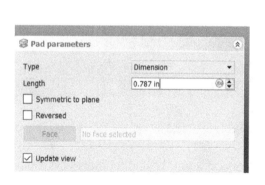
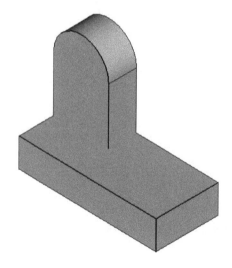

Creating the Rib

1. Activate the **Create Sketch** command and select the XZ_plane. Draw an inclined line, as shown.

2. Click **Sketch > View section** on the menu bar.

3. Click the **External geometry** 🗗 icon on the **Sketcher geometries** toolbar. Next, select the curved, vertical, and horizontal edges, as shown.

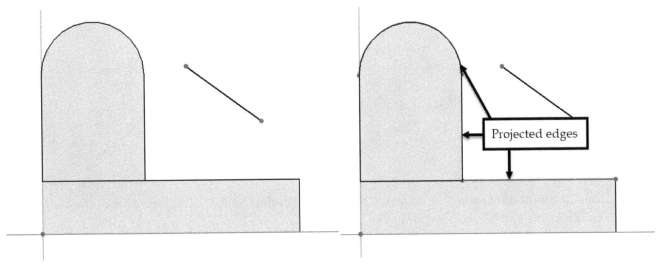

4. Create an arc and two lines, as shown.

5. Click the **Constrain equal** icon on the **Sketcher constraints** toolbar. Next, select the arc and curved edge.

6. Click the **Constrain coincident** icon on the **Sketcher constraints** toolbar. Next, select the endpoint of the arc and the endpoint of the curved edge.

7. Select the endpoint of the horizontal line and the endpoint of the horizontal edge.

8. On the **Sketcher constraints** toolbar, click **Constrain tangent**, and then select the inclined line and the arc; the line is made tangent to the arc.

9. Click the **Constrain coincident** icon on the **Sketcher constraints** toolbar. Next, select the lower endpoint of the inclined line and the endpoint of the horizontal line.

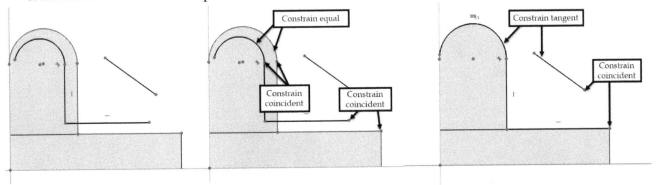

10. Click on the endpoint of the arc and drag it toward the right.

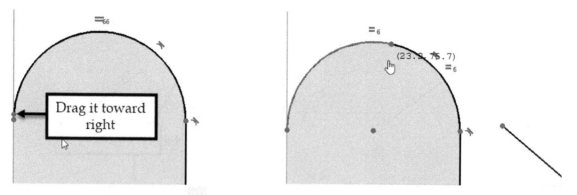

11. Click the **Constrain coincident** icon on the **Sketcher constraints** toolbar. Next, select the upper endpoint of the inclined line and the endpoint of the arc.

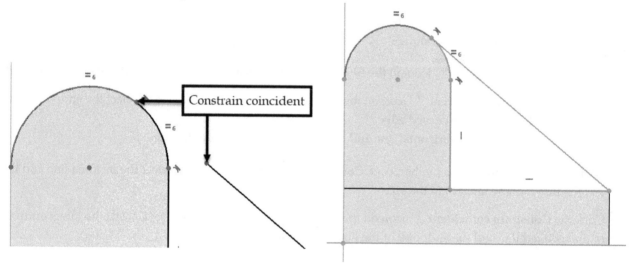

12. Click **Close** on the **Combo View** panel.

13. Click the **Pad** icon on the **Part Design Modeling** toolbar.

14. Type-in 0.394 in the **Length** box. Next, click **OK** to create the *Pad* feature.

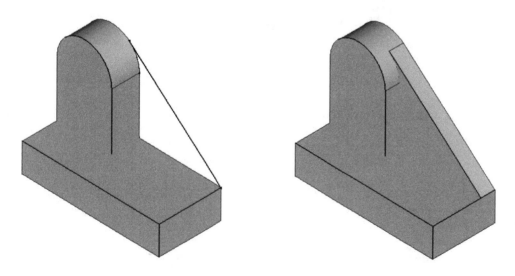

Creating the Extruded Cut features

1. Select the front face of the second feature and click the **Create Sketch** icon on the **Part Design Helper** toolbar.
2. On the **Sketcher geometries** toolbar, click the **Create slot** icon.
3. Click on the sketch plane to specify the first end of the slot. Next, move the pointer downward and click.
4. Click the **External geometry** icon on the **Sketcher geometries** toolbar.

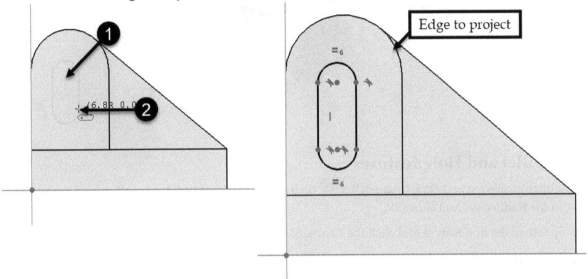

5. Click **Constrain coincident** on the **Sketcher constraints** toolbar. Next, select the center point of the projected curve edge and the centerpoint of the slot endcap.
6. Create the radius and vertical distance constraints, as shown.

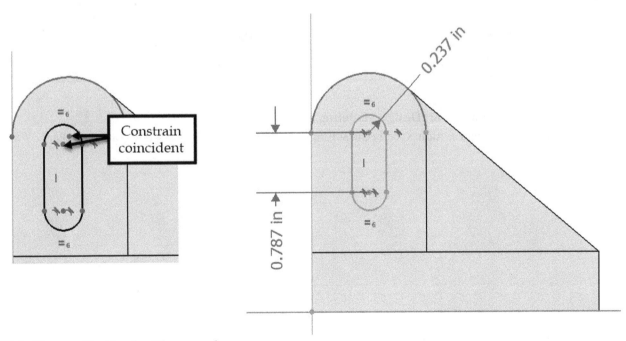

7. Click **Close** on the **Combo View** panel.
8. Click the **Pocket** icon on the **Part Design Modeling** toolbar.
9. On the **Pocket parameters** section, select **Type > Through all**. Next, click **OK**.

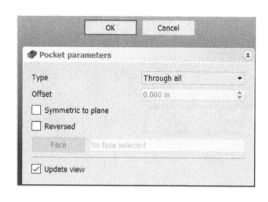

Creating the Fillet and Hole features

1. Select the right vertical edge and click **Create fillet** 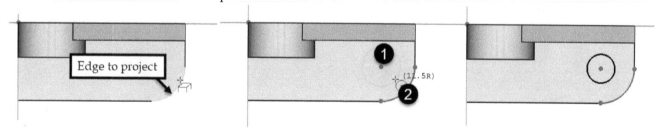 on the **Part Design Modeling** toolbar.
2. Type **0.787** in the **Radius** box and click **OK**.
3. Select the top face of the first feature and click the **Create Sketch** icon on the **Part Design Helper** toolbar.
4. Click **External geometry** on the **Sketcher geometries** toolbar. Next, select the curved edge, as shown.
5. Click the **Create circle** icon on the **Sketcher geometries** toolbar. Next, select the center point of the projected edge. Move the pointer outward and click to create a circle.
6. Click **Close** on the **Combo View** panel.

7. Click the **Hole** icon on the **Part Design Modeling** toolbar.
8. On the **Hole parameters** section, specify the settings, as shown. Next, click **OK** to create the hole.

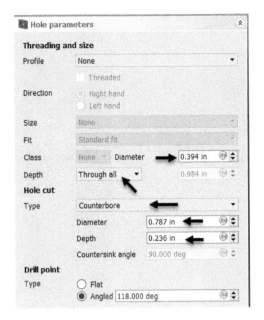

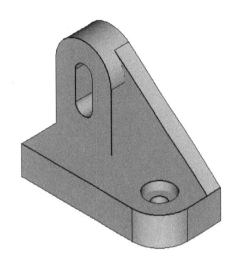

9. Select the front face of the rectangular base and click the **Create Sketch** icon on the **Part Design Helper** toolbar.

10. Draw a sketch and add dimensions to it. Click **Close** on the **Combo View** panel.

11. Create a *Pocket* feature using the sketch.

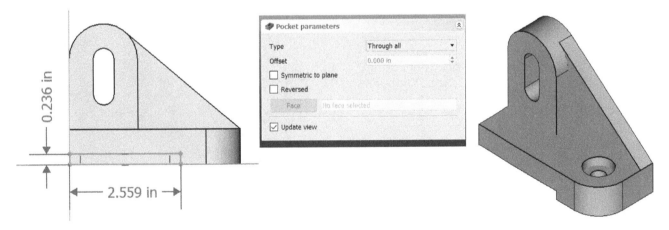

12. Save and close the part file.

Exercises

Exercise 1 (Millimetres)

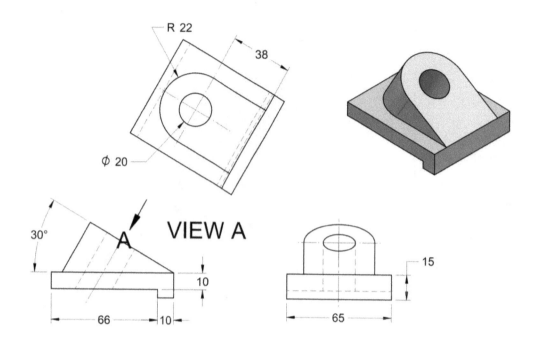

VIEW A

Exercise 2 (Inches)

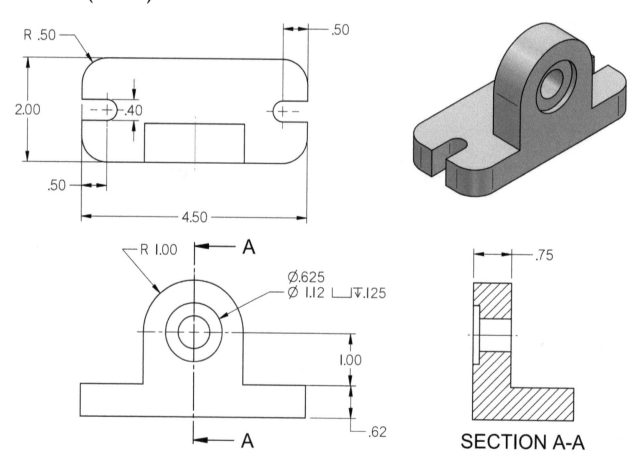

SECTION A-A

Exercise 3 (Millimeters)

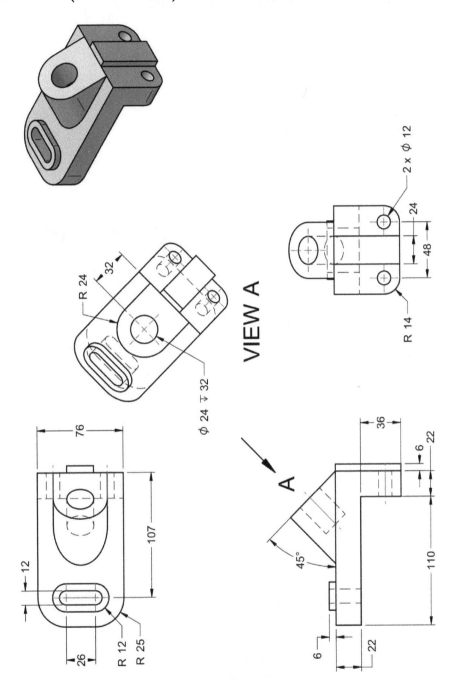

Chapter 5: Patterned Geometry

Tutorial 1

In this example, you create the part shown next.

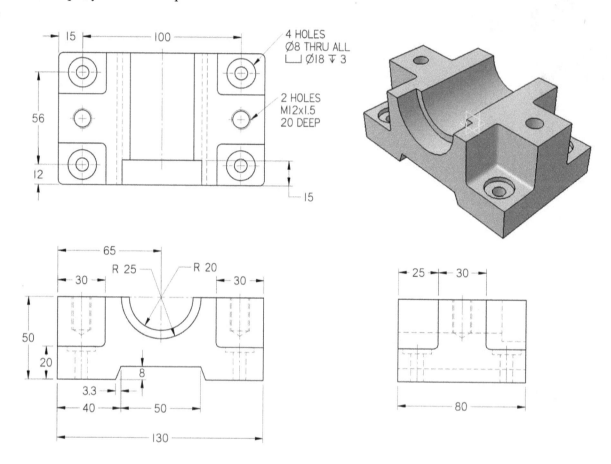

Creating a New document

1. Click **FreeCAD** on the desktop to start.
2. On the Home page, click **Documents > Create New**; it creates a new document.
3. On the **Workbench** toolbar, select **Workbench** drop-down **> Part Design**.
4. Click **Edit > Preferences** on the **Menu** bar; the **Preferences** dialog appears on the screen.
5. Click **Units** tab and select **User system > Standard (mm/kg/s/degree)**.
6. Select **Number of decimals > 2** and click **OK** on the **Preferences** dialog.

Creating the Extruded features

1. To start a sketch, click **Create Sketch** on the **Part Design Helper** toolbar.
2. Click on the XZ_Plane and click **OK** on the **Combo View**; the selected plane orients normal to the screen.
3. On the **Sketcher geometries** toolbar, click **Rectangle** . Next, specify the two corners of the rectangle.
4. Click the **Constrain symmetrical** icon on the **Sketcher constraints** toolbar. Next, select the lower right corner point of the rectangle.

5. Select the sketch origin point and the lower-left corner of the rectangle; the two corners of the rectangle are made symmetric about the sketch origin.
6. Add vertical and horizontal distance constraints to the rectangle.

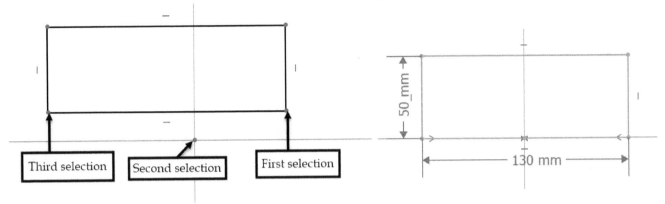

7. Click the **Close** button on the **Combo View** panel.
8. Activate the **Pad** tool on the **Part Design Modeling** toolbar.
9. On the **Pad parameters** section, check the **Symmetry to plane** option. Type **80** in the **Length** box and click **OK** to create the *Pad* feature.

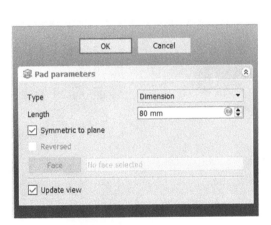

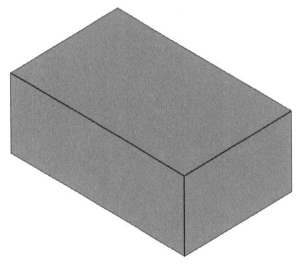

10. Select the top face of the model and click the **Create Sketch** icon on the **Part Design Helper** toolbar.
11. Click the **External geometry** icon on the **Sketcher geometries** toolbar.
12. Select the left vertical edge of the top face of the *Pad* feature, as shown. Next, create two rectangles.
13. Click the **Constrain coincident** icon on the **Sketcher constraints** toolbar.
14. Select the top-left corner point of the upper rectangle. Next, select the top endpoint of the projected edge; the two selected points are constrained coincidentally.
15. Likewise, constrain the bottom left corner point of the lower rectangle with the bottom point of the projected edge.
16. Click the **Constrain equal** icon on the **Sketcher constraints** toolbar. Next, select the inner horizontal lines of the two rectangles; they are constrained equally.
17. Select the right vertical lines of the two rectangles to constrain them equally.

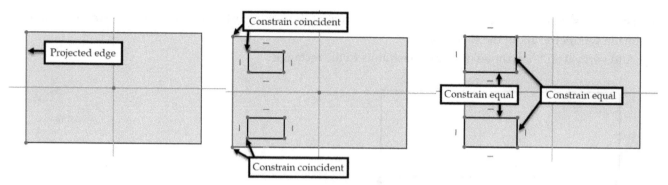

18. On the **Sketcher constraints** toolbar, click the **Constrain horizontal distance** icon.
19. Select the horizontal line and type-in **30** in the **Length** box on the **Insert Length** dialog, and then click **OK**.
20. Likewise, click the **Constrain vertical distance** icon on the **Sketcher constraints** toolbar.
21. Select the vertical line and type-in **25** in the **Length** box on the **Insert Length** dialog, and click **OK**.
22. Click the **Close** button on the **Combo View** panel.
23. Click the **Pocket** icon on the **Part Design Modeling** toolbar; the **Pocket parameters** section appears on the **Combo View** panel.
24. Type-in **30** in the **Length** box on the **Combo View** panel and click **OK** to create the *Pocket* feature.

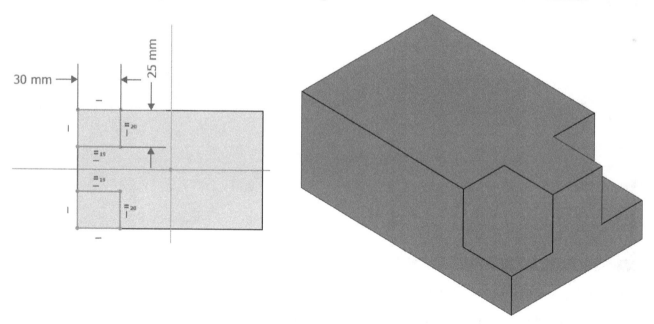

Creating the Hole features

1. Select the horizontal face of the *Pocket* feature and click the **Create Sketch** on the **Part Design Helper** toolbar.
2. On the **Sketcher geometries** toolbar, click the **External geometry** icon to project the edges.
3. Select the horizontal and vertical edges of the *Pocket* features, as shown.

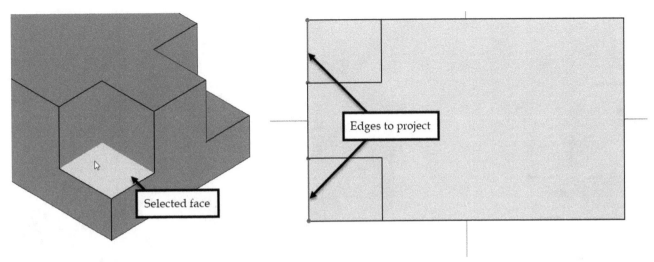

Selected face

Edges to project

4. Click the **Create circle** icon on the **Sketcher geometries** toolbar.
5. Create two circles and horizontal and vertical distance constraints, as shown.

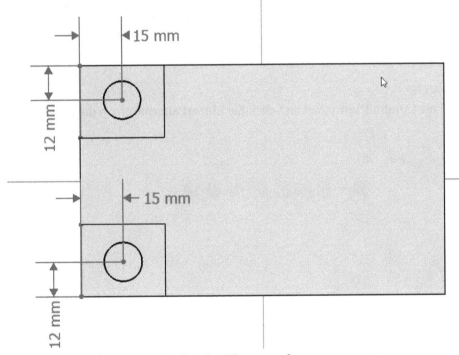

6. Click the **Close** button on the **Combo View** panel.

7. Click the **Hole** tool on the **Part Design Modeling** toolbar; the sketch is selected automatically.
8. Type-in **8** in the **Diameter** box and select **Depth > Through All**.
9. On the **Hole Parameters** section, under the **Hole cut**, select **Type > Counterbore**.
10. Type-in **18** and **3** in the **Diameter** and **Depth** boxes, respectively.
11. Under the **Drill point**, select **Type > Flat**.
12. Click **OK** on the **Combo View** panel; the counterbore hole is created.

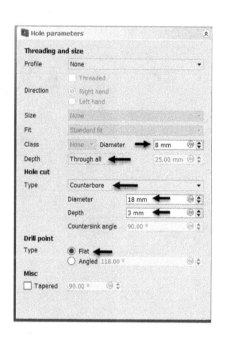

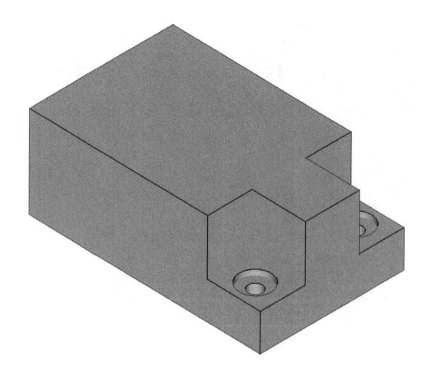

Creating the Linear Pattern

1. Select the **Pocket** feature from the **Combo View** panel and click the **LinearPattern** icon on the **Part Design Modeling** toolbar.

2. Click **Create Sketch** on the **Part Design Helper** toolbar.
3. Click the **Add feature** button on the **LinearPattern parameters** section and select the cylindrical face of the counterbore hole.
4. On the **LinearPattern parameters** section, select **Direction > Horizontal sketch axis**.
5. Type **100** and **2** in the **Length** and **Occurrences** boxes, respectively. Next, click **OK** to create the linear pattern.

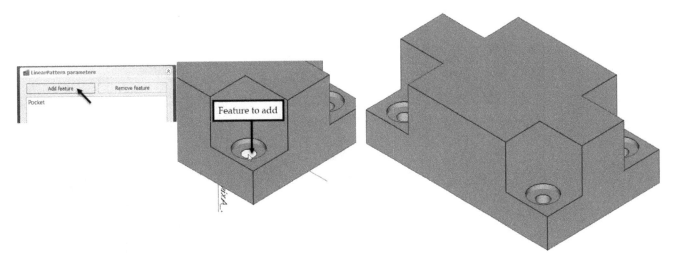

Creating the threaded Hole feature

1. Select the top face of the model and click the **Create Sketch** on the **Part Design Helper** toolbar.

2. Click the **External geometry** icon on the **Sketcher geometries** toolbar.

3. Select the left vertical edge of the part, as shown. Press **Esc** to deactivate the tool.

4. Click the **Create circle** icon on the **Sketcher geometries** toolbar.

5. Click on the horizontal sketch axis to define the center of the circle. Next, move the pointer outward and click to create a circle, as shown.

6. On the **Sketcher constraints** toolbar, click the **Constrain horizontal distance** tool.

7. Select the center point of the circle and the endpoint of the projected vertical edge, as shown.

8. Type-in **15** in the **Length** box of the **Insert Length** dialog and click **OK.**

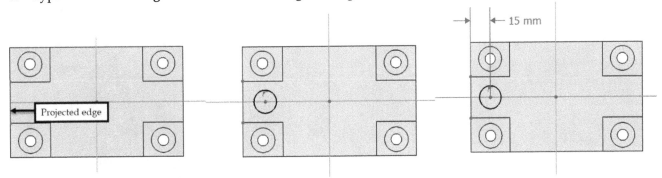

9. Click **Close** on the **Combo View** panel.

10. Click the **Hole** icon on the **Part Design Modeling** toolbar; the **Hole parameters** section appears on the screen.

11. Under the **Threading and size**, select **Profile > ISO metric coarse profile.**

12. Check the **Threaded** option, and then select **Direction > Right hand**.

13. Select **Size > M12** and **Class > 4G**.

14. Select **Depth > Dimension** and type-in **20** in the dimension box.

15. Under the **Drill point** section, select the **Type > Angled** option. Next, type **118** in the angle box.

16. Click **OK** on the **Combo View** panel.

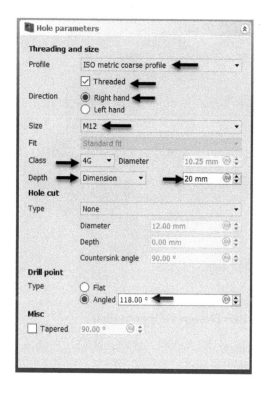

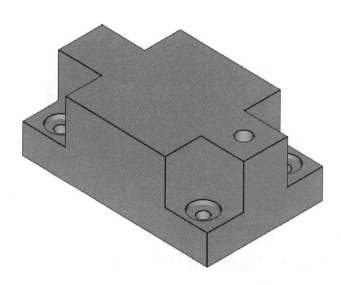

Mirroring the Features

1. On the **Part Design Modeling** toolbar, click the **Mirrored** icon.

2. Under the **Select feature** on the **Combo View**, select **Hole001** and click **OK**.
3. On the **Combo View** panel, select **Plane> Vertical sketch axis** option under the **Mirrored parameters** section.
4. Click **OK** to mirror the *Hole* feature.

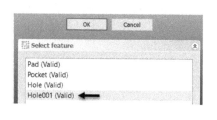

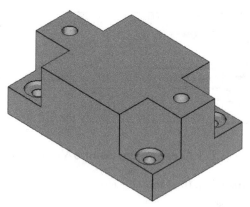

Creating the Hole and Pocket features

1. Select the front face of the part geometry and click the **Create Sketch** icon on the **Part Design Helper** toolbar.
2. Click the **External geometry** icon on the **Sketcher geometries** toolbar.
3. Select the top horizontal edge of the part, as shown. Press **Esc** to deactivate the tool.
4. Click the **Create circle** icon on the **Sketcher geometries** toolbar.

5. Click on the vertical sketch axis to define the center point of the circle. Move the pointer outward and click to create a circle.

6. Click the **Constrain point onto object** 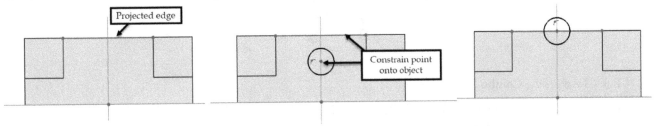 icon on the **Sketcher constraints** toolbar and select the center point of the circle. Next, select the projected edge.

7. Click **Close** on the **Combo View** panel.

8. Click the **Hole** icon on the **Part Design Modeling** toolbar.
9. On the **Hole parameters** section, select **Profile > None**.
10. Type 40 in the **Diameter** box. Next, select the **Depth > Through all**.
11. In the **Hole cut** section, select **Type > Counterbore**.
12. Type-in **50** and **15** in the **Diameter** and **Depth** boxes, respectively.
13. Click **OK** to create the counterbore hole.

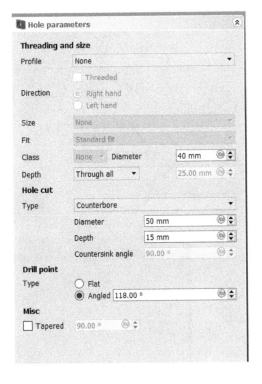

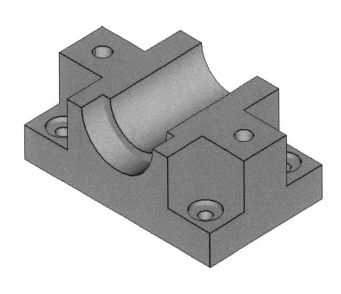

14. Select the front face of the part geometry and click the **Create Sketch** icon on the **Part Design Helper** toolbar.
15. Create a closed sketch using the Polyline command. Next, add vertical and horizontal distance constraints to it.
16. Click the **Constrain symmetrical** icon on the **Sketcher constraints** toolbar and select an endpoint of the lower horizontal line. Next, select the sketch origin.

17. Select the other endpoint of the lower horizontal line; the two endpoints of the lower horizontal line are made symmetric about the sketch origin.

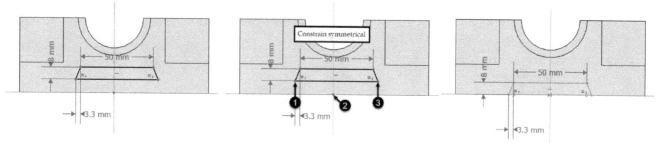

18. Click **Close** on the **Combo View** panel.
19. Click the **Pocket** 🔳 icon on the **Part Design Modeling** toolbar.
20. Select **Type > Through all** from the **Pocket parameters** section. Next, click **OK**.
21. On the **View** toolbar, select **Draw style > Wireframe**.
22. Press and hold the Ctrl key and select the internal edges of the pocket feature, as shown.
23. Press and hold the middle and right mouse buttons, and then drag the cursor.
24. Press and hold the Ctrl key and select the internal edges of the remaining pocket features.
25. Click the **Fillet** 🔳 icon on the **Part Design Modeling** toolbar. Next, type 2 in the **Radius** box and click **OK** to create the fillets.

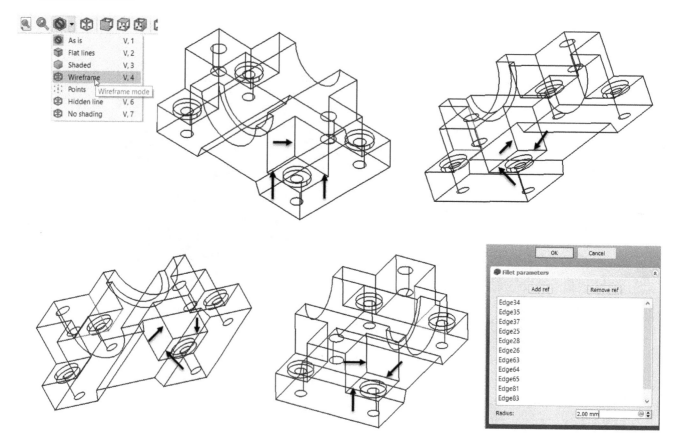

26. On the **View** toolbar, select **Draw style > Flat lines**.

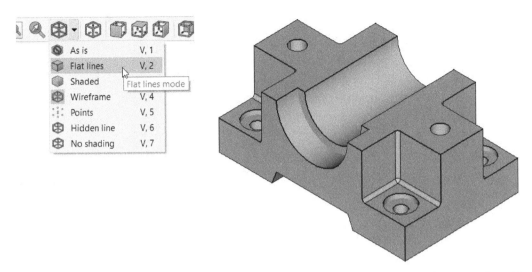

27. Click the **Save** icon on the **File** toolbar located at the top-left corner of the window. Next, type C5_exampl1 in the **File name** box, and then click **Save**.

28. Click **File > Close** on the menu bar to close the document.

Tutorial 2 (Millimetres)

In this example, you create the part shown next.

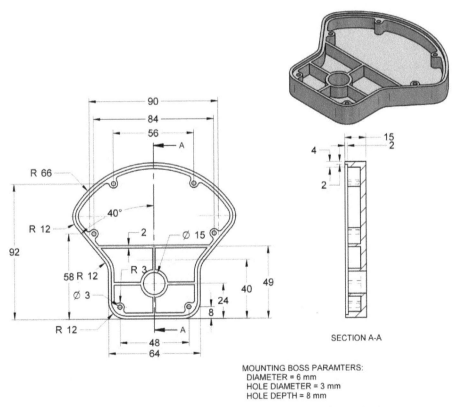

SECTION A-A

MOUNTING BOSS PARAMTERS:
DIAMETER = 6 mm
HOLE DIAMETER = 3 mm
HOLE DEPTH = 8 mm

FILLET MOUNTING BOSS CORNER 2 mm

Creating a New document

1. Click **FreeCAD** on the desktop to start.
2. On the Home page, click **Documents > Create New**; it creates a new document.
3. On the **Workbench** toolbar, select **Workbench** drop-down **> Part Design**.
4. Click **Edit > Preferences** on the **Menu** bar; the **Preferences** dialog appears on the screen.
5. Click **Units** tab and select **User system > Standard (mm/kg/s/degree)**.
6. Select **Number of decimals > 2** and click **OK** on the **Preferences** dialog.

Creating the Extruded Feature

1. Click the **Create a new Sketch** command on the **Part Design Helper** Toolbar and start a new sketch on the **XY** plane.

2. On the **Sketcher geometries** toolbar, click the **Create polyline** command and draw the sketch, as shown in the figure below.

3. On the **Sketcher geometries** toolbar, click the **Arc** drop-down **> Create arc by three points** command, and then create an arc by specifying the points in the sequence, as shown.

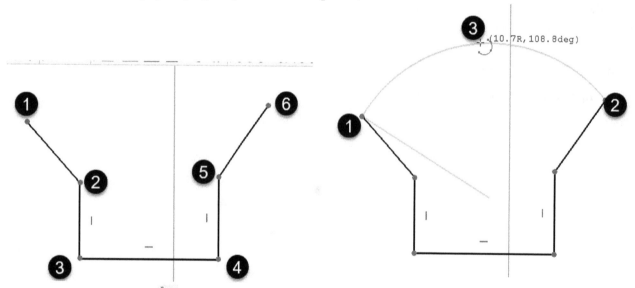

4. Click the **Create Fillet** command on the **Part tools** Toolbar, and then select the sharp corners to fillet.
5. Select the arc and the inclined line connected to it; the fillet is created at the corner.
6. Likewise, select the arc and the inclined line connected to it at the other end.

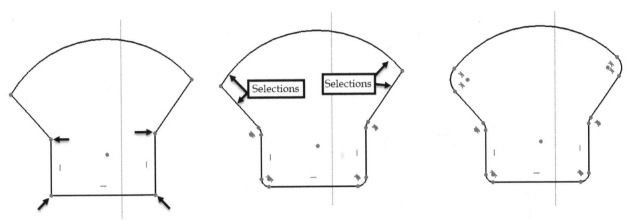

7. Click the **Constrain equal** ▬ icon on the **Sketcher constraints** toolbar. Next, apply the Equal constraint between the fillets, as shown.

8. Apply the **Equal** constraint between the fillets, as shown.

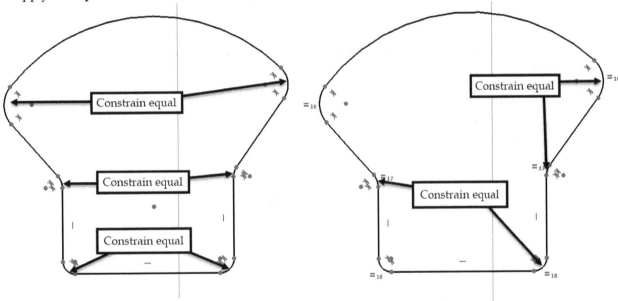

9. Apply the **Equal** constraint between the two vertical lines.

10. Apply the **Equal** constraint between the two inclined lines. Next, right click in the graphics window.

11. Select the centerpoints of the two fillets, as shown. Next, click the **Constrain horizontal** ▬ icon on the **Sketcher constraints** toolbar.

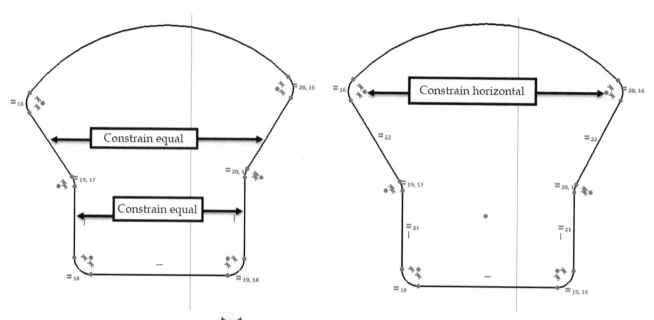

12. Click the **Constrain symmetrical** ✕ icon on the **Sketcher constraints** toolbar and select the points in the sequence, as shown.

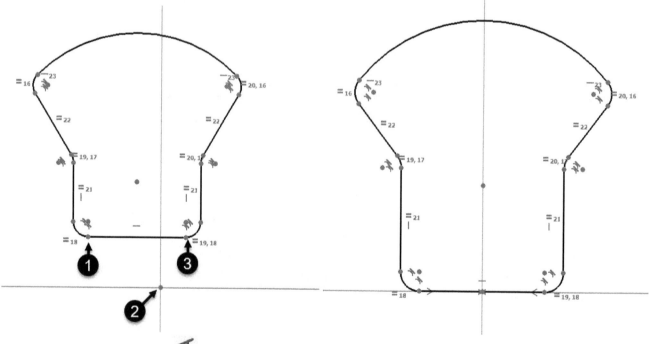

13. Click the **Constrain angle** ◁ icon on the **Sketcher constraints** toolbar. Next, select the left inclined and vertical lines, as shown. Type **140** in the **Angle** box and click **OK**.

14. Apply the dimensional constraints to the sketch, as shown. Do not change the values.

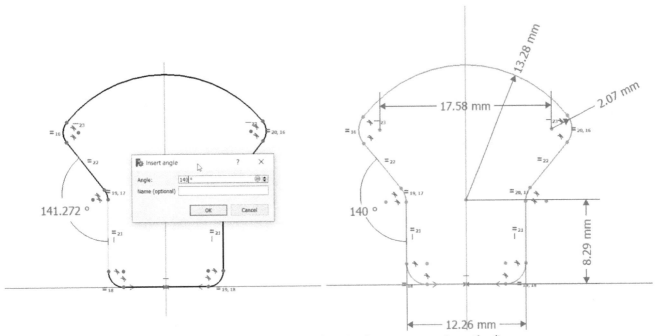

15. Double-click on the constraints and change their values in the sequence given the figure.

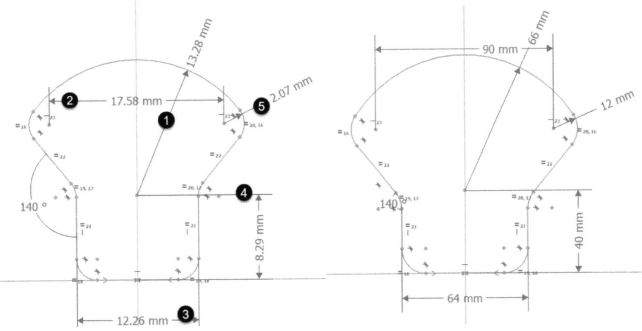

16. Click the **Close** button on the **Combo View** panel.

17. Activate the **Pad** command. Next, type-in **14** in the **Length** box under the **Pad parameters** section of the **Combo View**.

18. Click **OK** to create the *Pad* feature.

19. Select the top face of the pad feature and click the **Thickness** icon on the **Part Design Modeling** toolbar.

20. Type-in **4** in the **Thickness** box on the **Thickness parameters** section.

21. Check the **Make thickness inwards** option and click **OK**.

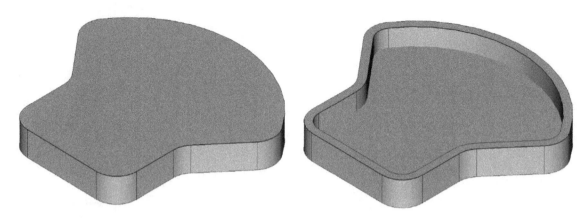

Adding a Lip to the model

1. In the **Combo View** panel, expand the **Origin** node and select the YZ Plane.

2. Click the **Create Sketch** icon on the **Part Design Helper** toolbar.

3. Click the **View Section** icon on the **Part Design Helper** toolbar.

4. Click **External geometry** on the **Sketcher geometries** toolbar, and then select the internal vertical edge.

5. Click the **Create rectangle** icon on the **Sketcher geometries** toolbar.

6. Select the top endpoint of the projected edge. Next, move the pointer toward the bottom left corner and click.

7. Add Vertical distance and Horizontal distance constraints to the rectangle, as shown.

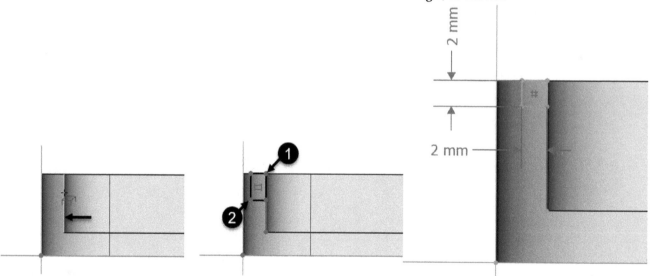

8. Click **Close** on the **Combo View** panel.

9. In the **Combo View** panel, expand the **Pad** feature and select the **Sketch**.

10. In the **Properties** panel, scroll down and click the drop-down next to the **Visibility** property. Next, select **true** from the drop-down; the sketch used for the Pad feature is visible in the graphics window.

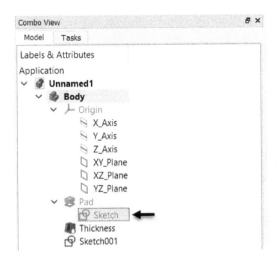
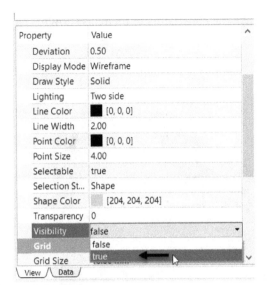

11. Click in the graphics area to deselect the sketch of the Pad feature.

12. Click the **Subtractive Pipe** 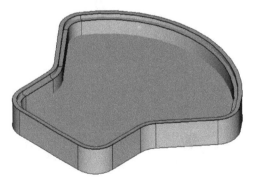 icon on the **Part Design Modeling** toolbar; the sketch created on the YZ plane is selected as the profile.

13. Press and hold middle and right mouse buttons. Next, drag the cursor such that the bottom face of the model is displayed.

14. On the **Pipe parameters** section, click the **Object** button under **Pipe to sweep along** section.

15. Select the sketch used for the *Pad* feature. Next, click **OK** to create the subtractive pipe feature.

16. Click the **Set to isometric view**  icon on the **View** toolbar to change the view to isometric.

Creating Bosses

1. Click on the horizontal face create by the subtractive pipe feature. Next, click the **Create sketch** icon on the **Part Design Helper** toolbar.

2. Draw the three circles on the sketch plane. Next, click **Constrain equal** ═ on the **Sketcher constraints** toolbar.

3. Select the first two circles to make them equal in diameter. Next, select the second and third circles to make them equal.

4. Add dimensional constraints to them, as shown.

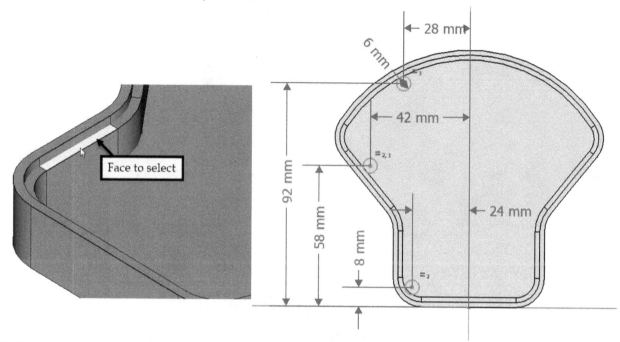

5. Click the **Create circle** icon on the **Sketcher geometries** toolbar. Next, select any one of the centerpoints of the circles. Move the pointer outward and click to create a circle.
6. Likewise, create two more circles concentric to the other two circles.

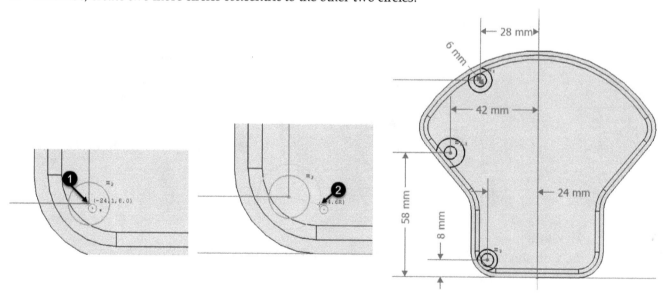

7. Click the **Constrain equal** ═ icon on the **Sketcher constraints** toolbar and select two new circles; the two circles are made equal in diameter.
8. Likewise, make the third new circle equal to the second new circle.
9. Click the **Constrain diameter** ⌀ icon on the **Sketcher constraints** toolbar and select any one of the new circles.
10. Type 3 in the **Diameter** box and click **OK**.

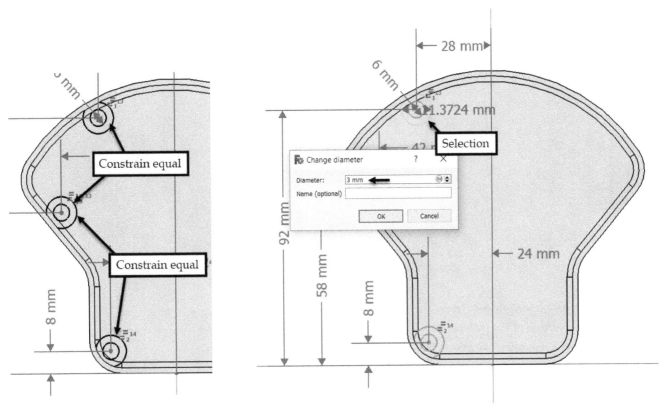

11. Click the **Close** button on the **Combo View** panel.
12. On the **Part Design Modeling** toolbar, click the **Pad** icon.
13. On the **Pad parameters** section, enter **8** in the **Length** box. Next, check the **Reversed** option and click **OK**.

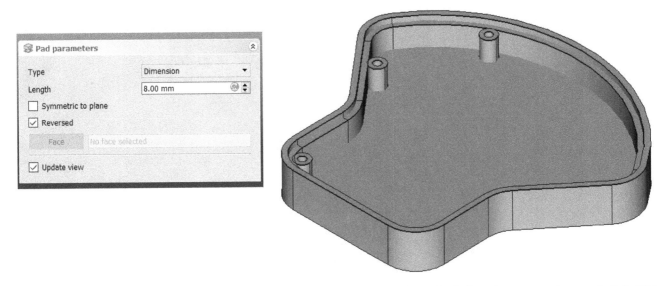

14. On the toolbar, click the **Mirror** command. Next, select **Pad001** from the **Select feature** section, and click **OK**.
15. Select **Base YZ plane** from the **Plane** drop-down, and click **OK**.

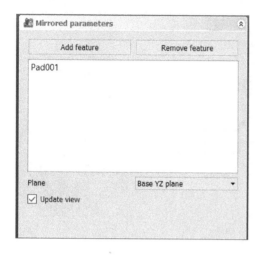

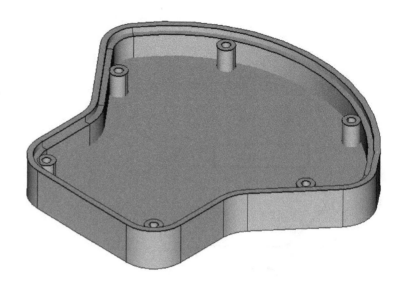

16. Click **View > Draw Style > Wireframe** on the Menu bar.
17. Zoom-in to anyone of the pad features. Next, press and hold the Ctrl key and select the edges where the pad feature meets the wall of the geometry.
18. Click the **Create fillet** icon on the **Part Design Modeling** toolbar. Next, type 1 in the **Radius** box and click **OK**.

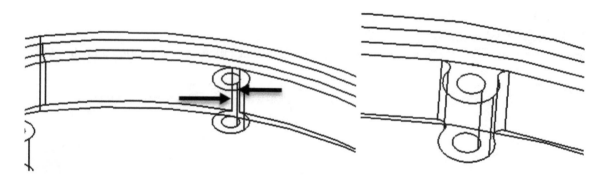

19. Likewise, create fillets for the remaining pad features.
20. Click **View > Draw style > Flat lines** on the menu bar.

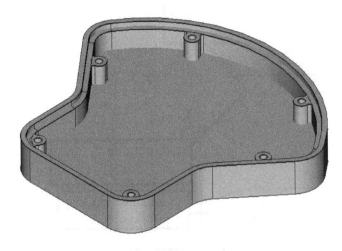

Creating Ribs

1. Select the bottom face of the shell feature and click **Create sketch** on the **Part Design Helper** toolbar.

2. Click the **External geometry** icon on the **Sketcher geometries** toolbar. Next, select the edges of the model, as shown,

3. Click the **Center and rim point** command on the **Sketcher geometries** toolbar and create two circles, as shown.

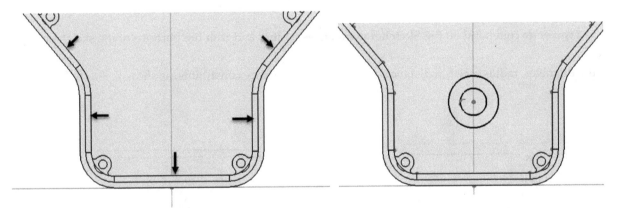

4. Click the **Polyline** command on the **Sketcher geometries** toolbar and create the lines, as shown.

5. On the **Sketcher constraints** toolbar, click **Constrain point onto object**. Next, constrain the endpoints of the lines onto the projected edges, as shown.

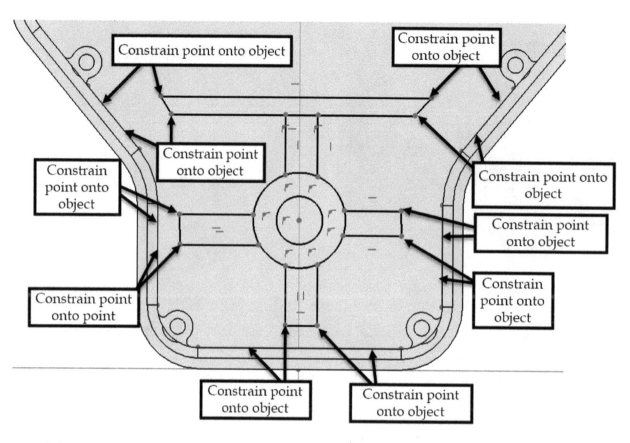

6. Click the **Trim edge** command on the **Sketcher geometries** toolbar and trim the portions of the sketch, as shown.

7. Create the diameter, radius, vertical distance, and horizontal distance constraints, as shown.

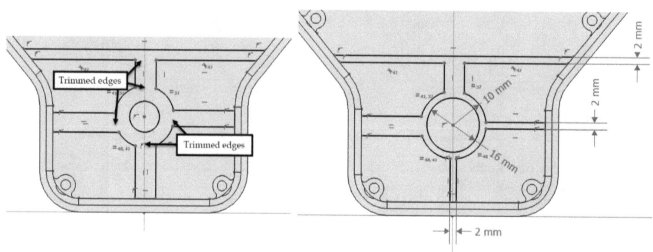

8. Apply the horizontal and vertical constraints between the endpoints of the lines, as shown.

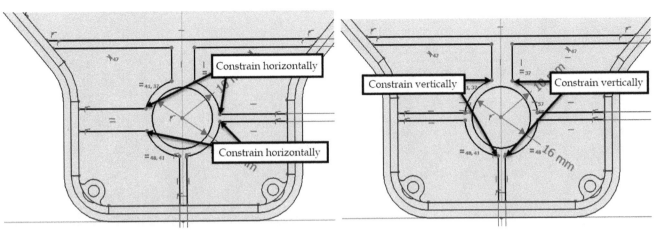

9. Create vertical distance and horizontal distance constraints, as shown.

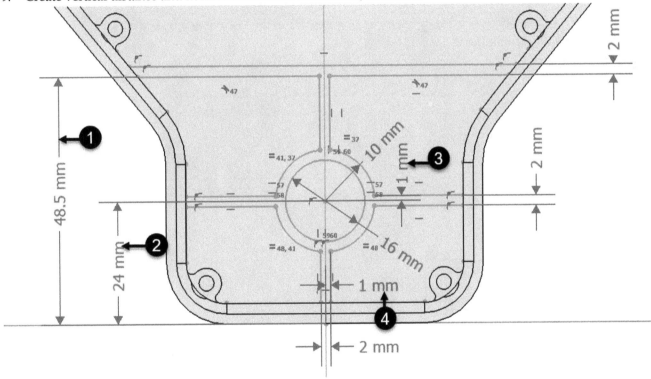

10. Click the **Close** button on the **Combo View** panel.
11. Click the **Pad** icon on the **Part Design Modeling** toolbar. Next, select **Type > Up to face** from the **Pad parameters** section.
12. Select the horizontal face of the Subtractive pipe feature. Next, click **OK**.

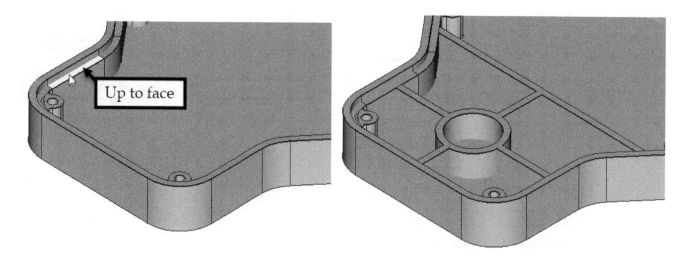

13. Click **File > Save** on the menu bar. Next, type **C7_example1** in the **File name** box, and click Save.

14. Click **File > Close** on the menu bar.

Exercises

Exercise 1

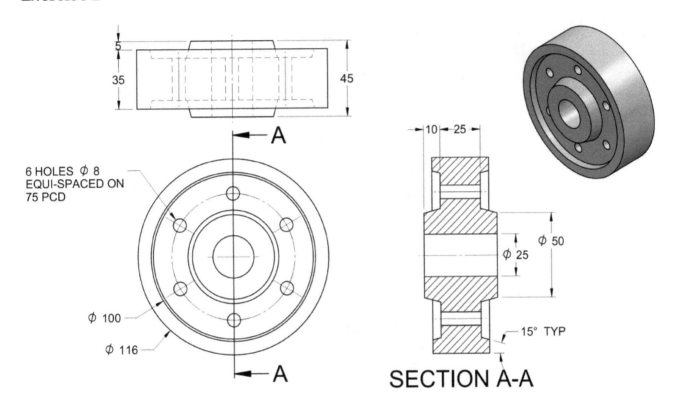

6 HOLES Ø 8
EQUI-SPACED ON
75 PCD

Ø 100

Ø 116

SECTION A-A

Exercise 2

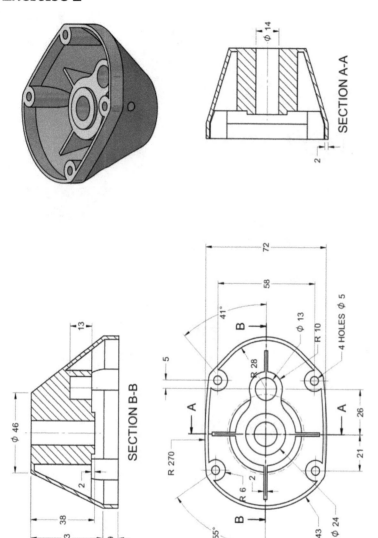

Chapter 6: Sweep Features

Tutorial 1

In this example, you create the part shown below.

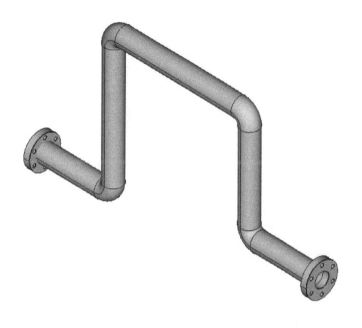

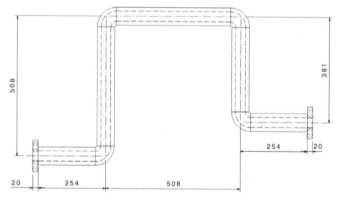

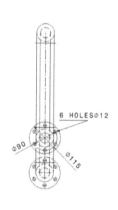

PIPE I.D. 51

PIPE O.D. 65

Creating a New document

1. Click **FreeCAD** on the desktop to start.
2. On the Home page, click **Documents > Create New**; it creates a new document.
3. On the **Workbench** toolbar, select **Workbench** drop-down **> Part Design**.
4. Click **Edit > Preferences** on the **Menu** bar; the **Preferences** dialog appears on the screen.
5. Click **Units** tab and select **User system > Standard (mm/kg/s/degree)**.
6. Select **Number of decimals > 2** and click **OK** on the **Preferences** dialog.

Creating the Sweep Feature

1. Click **Create Sketch** 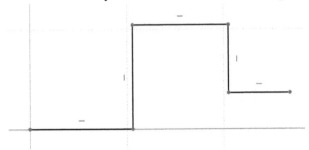 command on the **Part Design Helper** toolbar and then select **XZ_plane**.
2. Click **OK** on the **Combo View** plane.
3. Click the **Polyline** icon on the **Sketcher geometries** toolbar. Next, create the lines, as shown.

4. On the **Sketcher geometries** toolbar, click the **Create fillet** . Select the corner points of the sketch.

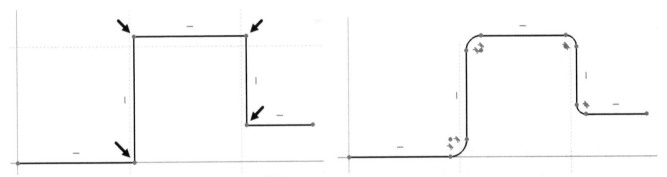

5. Click the **Constrain horizontal distance** icon on the **Sketcher constraints** toolbar.
6. Select the lower horizontal line of the sketch. Click **OK** on the **Insert Length** dialog.
7. Likewise, create the horizontal distance constraints, as shown.

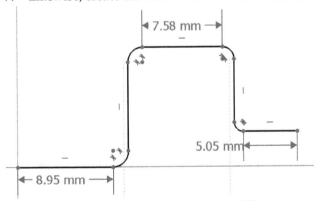

8. Click the **Constrain vertical distance** icon on the **Sketcher constraints** toolbar.
9. Select the left vertical line and click **OK** on the **Insert Length** dialog.
10. Likewise, select the right vertical line and **OK** on the **Insert Length** dialog.

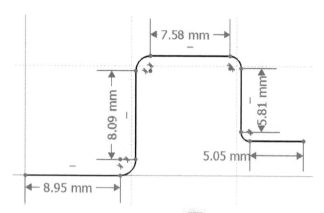

11. Click the **Constrain equal** icon on the **Sketcher constraints** toolbar. Select all the fillets.
12. Again, select the first and last fillets.

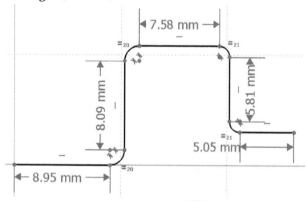

13. Click the **Constraint radius** on the **Sketcher constraints** toolbar.
14. Select any one fillet and click **OK** on the **Insert Length** dialog.

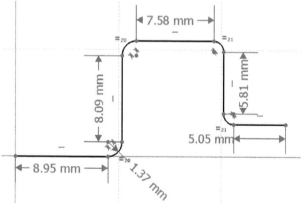

15. Double-click on the left vertical dimension and type-in **432** in the **Length** box on the **Insert Length** dialog.
16. Click **OK** to edit the dimension.
17. Likewise, edit all the values of the dimensions, as shown in the figure.

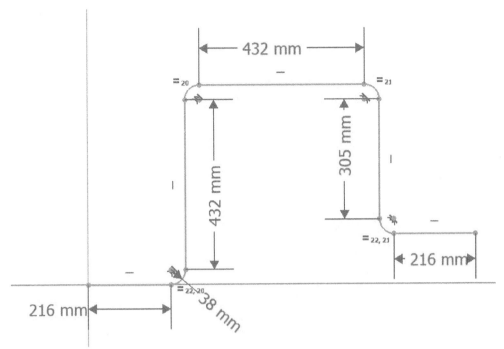

18. Click the **Close** button on the **Combo View** panel.

19. On the **Part Design Helper** toolbar, click the **Create a datum plane** ◇ icon.

20. Select the right horizontal line of the sketch to define the first reference.

21. Select the endpoint of the horizontal line to define the second reference.

22. Select **Normal to edge** from the **Attachment mode** section and click OK.

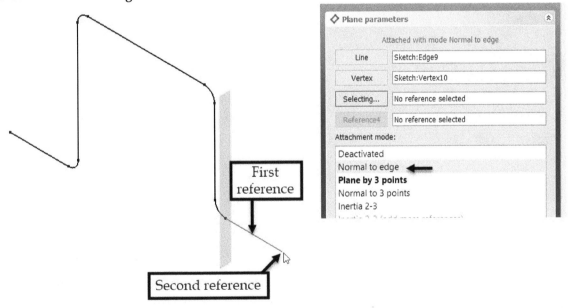

23. Click the **Create Sketch** 🗗 icon on the **Part Design Helper** toolbar. Next, select the newly created datum plane and click **OK**.

24. Click the **Create circle** ◉ tool on the **Sketcher geometries** toolbar.

25. Change the view orientation to the Isometric view. (on the graphics area, click the **Camera and render options > Isometric** from the right-side).
26. Click on the sketch origin to define the center point of the circle.
27. Move the pointer outward and click to create a circle.
28. Again, click on the sketch origin to define the center point of the circle.

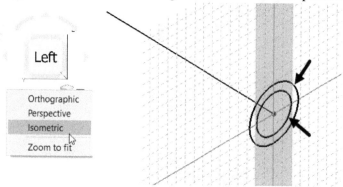

29. Move the pointer and click to create another circle. Make sure that the center points of the circles coincident with each other.
30. On the **Sketcher constraints** toolbar, click the **Constrain an arc or circle** drop-down and select **Constrain diameter**.
31. Select the inner circle. Next, type-in **51** in the **Length** box and click **OK** on the **Insert Length** dialog.
32. Select the outer circle. Next, type-in **65** in the **Length** box and click **OK** on the **Insert Length** dialog.

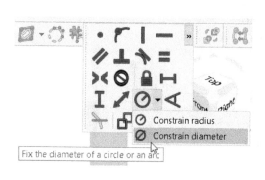
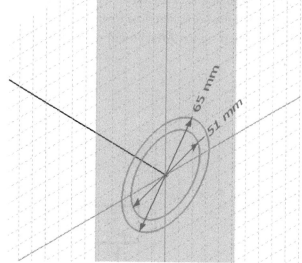

33. Click the **Close** button on the **Combo View** panel.
34. On the **Part Design Modeling** toolbar, click the **Additive pipe** icon. Next, select the **Sketch001** from the **Select feature** section on the **Combo View** panel.
35. Click **OK** on the **Combo View** panel.
36. Under the **Pipe parameters** section on the **Combo View**, click the **Object** button under the **Path to sweep along** section.
37. Select the first sketch from the graphics area and click **OK** to create the *Sweep* feature.

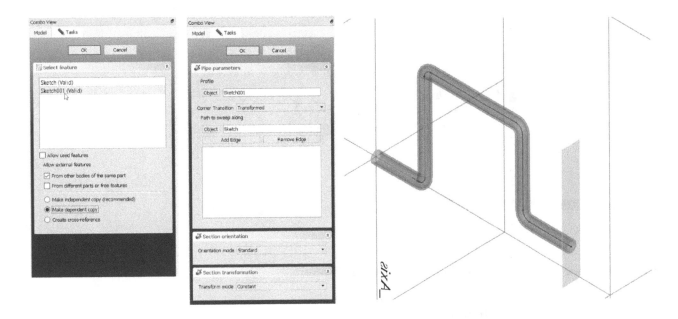

Adding the Extruded Feature

1. Click the **Create Sketch** command on the **Sketcher geometries** Toolbar.
2. Click on the datum plane displayed on the front-end face of the *Sweep* feature.
3. Change the view orientation to the Isometric view. (on the graphics area, click the **Camera and render options > Isometric** from the right-side).
4. Create two circles that are concentric with each other.
5. Click the **Constrain coincident** icon on the **Sketcher constraints** toolbar. Next, select the centerpoint of the circles and the sketch origin.
6. Click the **Constrain radius** drop-down and select the **Constrain diameter** icon on the **Sketcher constraints** toolbar.

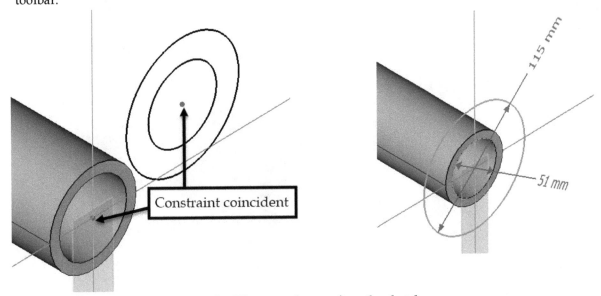

7. Click the **Close** button on the **Combo View** panel to confirm the sketch.
8. Activate the **Pad** command; the sketch is selected automatically.
9. Type-in **20** in the **Length** box under the **Pad parameters** section on the **Combo View** panel. N

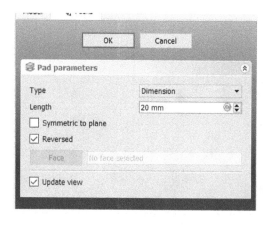

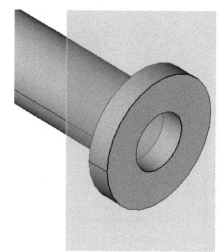

10. Click **OK** on the **Combo View** panel to complete the *Pad* feature.

Creating the Circular Pattern

1. Select the face of the pad feature and activate the **Create Sketch** command.
2. Click the **Create circle** icon on the **Sketcher geometries** toolbar. Next, click the vertical sketch axis and move the pointer outward. Again, click to create a circle.
3. On the **Sketcher constraints** toolbar, click **Constrain radius** drop-down > **Constrain diameter**.
4. Select the circle and enter 12 in the **Diameter** box. Next, click **OK** to add a diameter constraint.
5. Click the **Constrain vertical** icon on the **Sketcher constraints** toolbar. Next, select the sketch origin and the centerpoint of the circle.
6. Type **45** in the **Length** box and click **OK**.

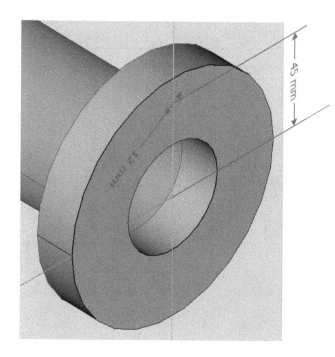

7. Click the **Close** button on the **Combo View** panel.
8. Click the **Pocket** icon on the **Part Design Modeling** toolbar.
9. Select **Type > To first** on the **Pocket parameters** section of the **Combo View** panel. Next, click **OK**.

10. Click the **Create a polar pattern feature** command on the **Part Tools** toolbar.
11. Select the **Pocket** from the **Select feature** panel. Next, click **OK**.
12. Under the **PolarPattern parameters** section and select **Axis > Normal sketch axis**.
13. Type-in **360** and **6** in the **Angle** and **Occurrences** boxes, respectively.
14. Click **OK** to create the pattern.

15. Create the *Pad*, *Pocket*, and *Polar pattern* features on the other end of the model.

 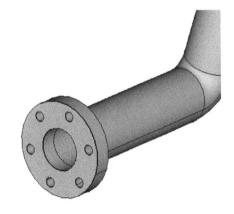

16. Click **File > Save** on the menu bar. Next, type C6_example1 in the **File name** box and click the **Save** button.
17. Click **File > Close** to close the document.

Exercises
Exercise1

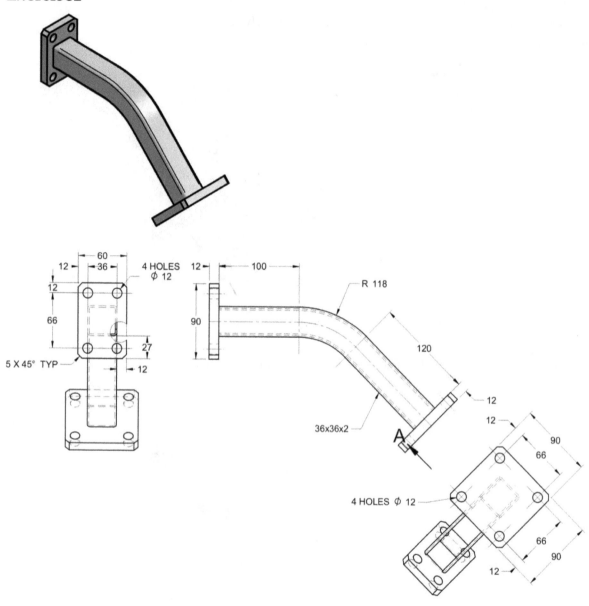

Chapter 7: Loft Features

Tutorial 1

In this example, you create the part shown below.

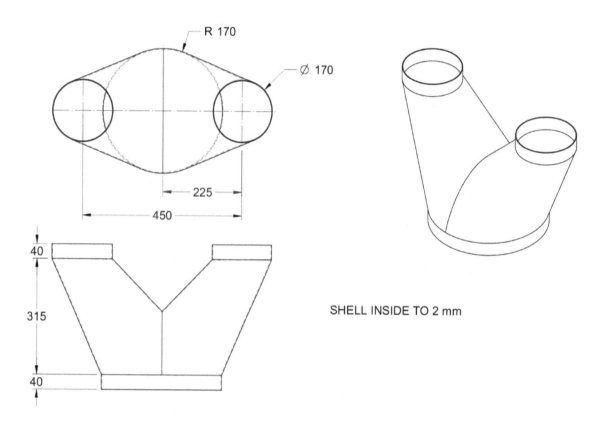

SHELL INSIDE TO 2 mm

Creating a New document

1. Click **FreeCAD** on the desktop to start.
2. On the Home page, click **Documents > Create New**; it creates a new document.
3. On the **Workbench** toolbar, select **Workbench** drop-down **> Part Design**.
4. Click **Edit > Preferences** on the **Menu** bar; the **Preferences** dialog appears on the screen.
5. Click **Units** tab and select **User system > Standard (mm/kg/s/degree)**.
6. Select **Number of decimals > 2** and click **OK** on the **Preferences** dialog.

Creating a Loft Feature

1. On the **Part Design Helper** toolbar, click the **Create Sketch** icon. Select the XY_Plane and click **OK**.
2. Draw two circles of **338** and **340** mm diameters. Next, click the **Close** button on the **Combo View** panel.
3. Click the **Model** tab on the **Combo View** panel. Next, expand the **Origin** node and select the **XY_Plane**.
4. On the **Part Design Helper** tool, click the **Create a new datum plane** ◇ tool.
5. Type **315** in the **Z** box of the **Attachment Offset** section. Next, click **OK**.

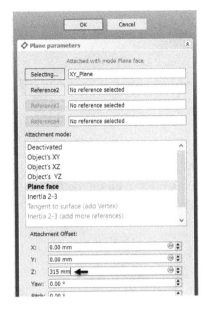
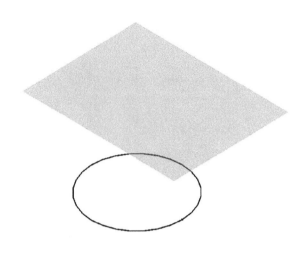

6. Click the **OK** button on the **Combo View** panel.
7. Select the newly created datum plane and click the **Create Sketch** icon on the **Part Design Helper** toolbar.
8. Draw two circles of **168** and **170** mm diameters and add constraints to them, as shown.
9. Click the **Close** button on the **Combo View** panel. Click in the graphics window to deselect the circle.

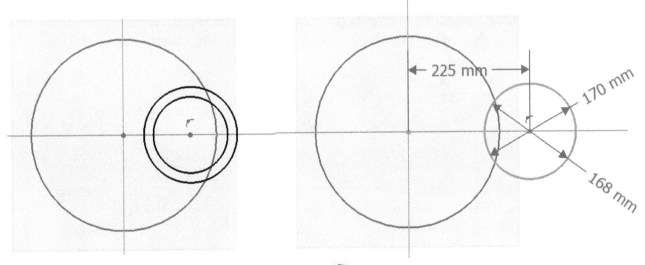

10. On the **Part Design Modeling** toolbar, click the **Loft** 🗔 icon. Select **Sketch001** from the **Select feature** section of the **Combo View** panel. Next, click **OK**.
11. Click the **Add section** button on the **Loft parameters** section and select the circle from the graphics window.
12. Click **OK**.

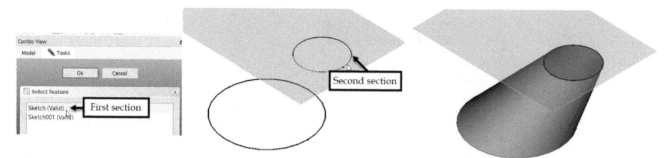

13. In the **Combo View** panel, expand the **AdditiveLoft** feature and select the first sketch.
14. Click the **Pad** icon on the **Part Design Modeling** toolbar. Next, check the Reversed option.
15. Enter **40** in the **Length** box and click **OK** to create a pad feature.

16. In the **Combo View** panel, expand the **AdditiveLoft** feature and select the second sketch.
17. Click the **Pad** icon on the **Part Design Modeling** toolbar. Next, enter **40** in the **Length** box and click **OK**.

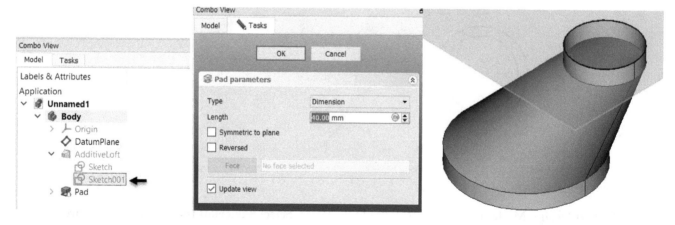

Mirroring the Loft and Pad features

1. On the **Part Design Modeling** toolbar, click the **Mirrored** icon. Next, select the **AdditiveLoft** feature from the **Select feature** section, and then click **OK**.
2. Select the *Pad* feature from the graphics window. Next, click the **Add feature** button on the **Mirrored parameters** section.
3. Select the **Base YZ plane** option from the **Plane** drop-down
4. Click **OK** mirror the *Loft* and *Pad* features.

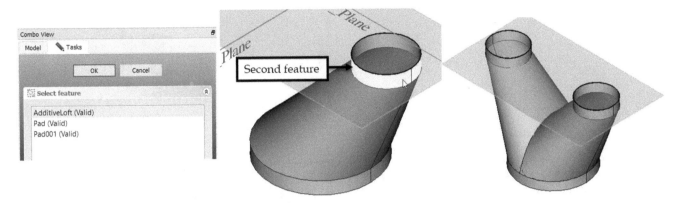

5. Click **File > Save** on the Menu bar. Next, enter C6_example2 in the **File name** box. Click **Save** to save the document

6. Click **File > Close** to close the document.

Exercises

Exercise 1

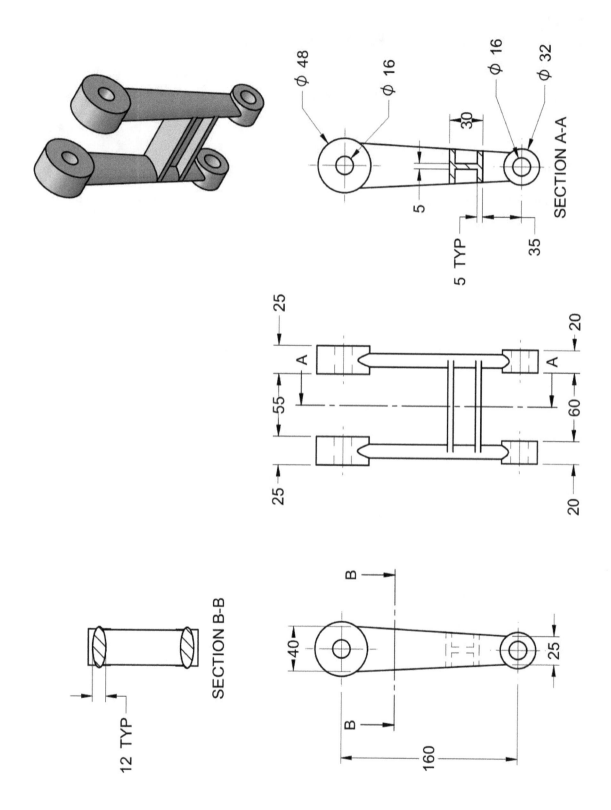

Chapter 8: Modifying Parts

Tutorial 1 (Inches)

In this example, you create the part shown below and then modify it.

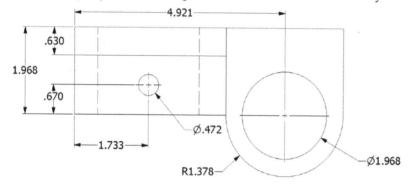

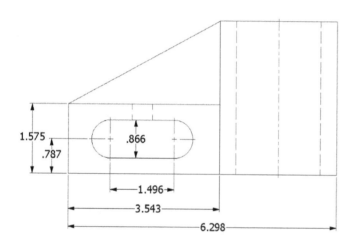

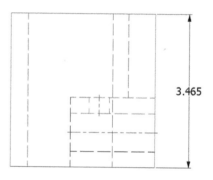

Creating a New document

1. Click **FreeCAD** on the desktop to start.
2. On the Start page, click **Documents > Create New**; it creates a new document.
3. On the **Workbench** toolbar, select **Workbench** drop-down **> Part Design**.
4. Click **Edit > Preferences** on the **Menu** bar; the **Preferences** dialog appears on the screen.
5. Click **Units** tab and select **User system > Imperial decimal**.
6. Select **Number of decimals > 3** and click **OK** on the **Preferences** dialog.
7. Create the part using the tools and commands available in FreeCAD, as shown in the figure. You can also download this file from the companion website.

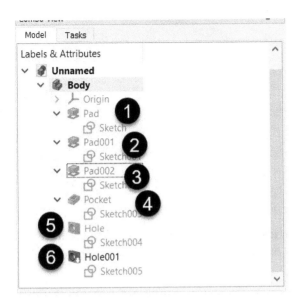

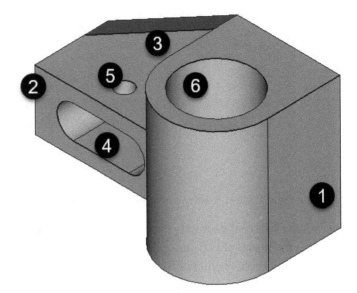

Editing a Feature

1. Click the right mouse button on the **Hole001** in the **Model** tab of the **Combo View** panel. Next, select **Edit hole** from the menu.
2. On the **Hole parameters** section, enter **1.378** in the **Diameter** box.
3. Select **Type > Counterbore** from the **Hole cut** section. Next, enter **1.968** and **0.787** in the **Diameter** and **Depth** boxes available under the **Hole cut** section, respectively.
4. Click **OK**.

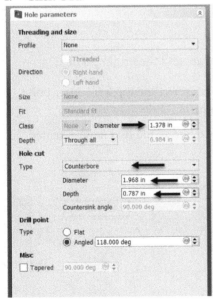

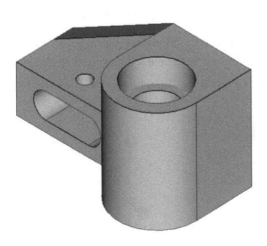

Editing Sketches

1. Expand the **Pad001** feature in the **Model** tab of the **Combo View** panel. Next, right-click on the *Sketch001* in and select **Edit sketch**. Modify the sketch, as shown. Click **Close** on the **Combo View** panel.

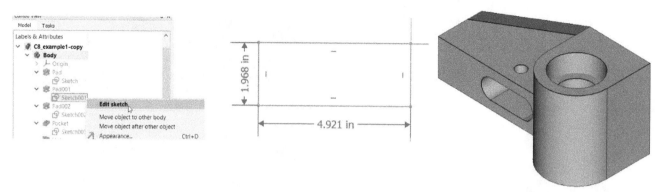

2. Expand the **Pocket** feature and right the mouse button on *Sketch003*. Next, select **Edit sketch**.

3. Click the **External geometry** icon on the **Sketcher geometries** toolbar. Next, select the left vertical edge.

4. Delete the horizontal distance constraint of the slot, as shown. Next, add a horizontal distance constraint between the center point of the left arc.

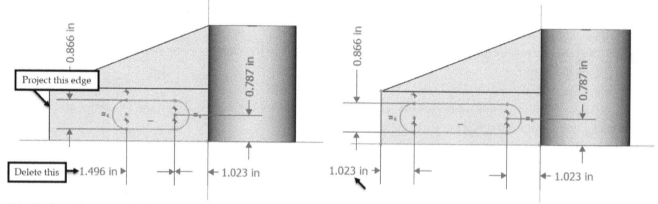

5. Delete the vertical distance constraint between the centerpoint of the right arc and the origin point.

6. Click the **Create polyline** icon on the **Sketcher geometries** toolbar. Next, select the top left corner point.

7. Select the centerpoint of the left arc. Next, select the bottom left corner point.

8. Click the **Constrain equal** icon on the **Sketcher constraints** toolbar. Next, select the two newly created lines.

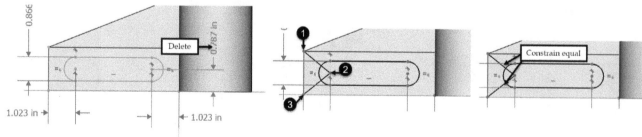

9. Select the two new lines, and click the **Toggle Construction geometry** icon on the **Sketcher geometries** toolbar.

10. Click **Close** on the **Combo View** panel.

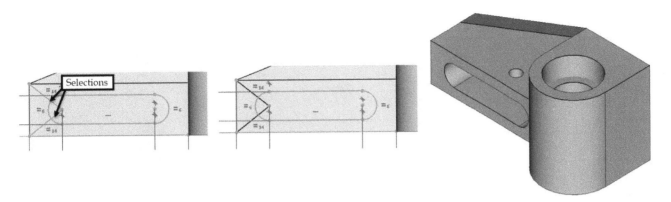

11. In the **Model** tab of the **Combo View** panel, expand the first **Hole** and click the right mouse button on the Sketch. Next, select **Edit sketch** from the menu.
12. Delete the vertical and horizontal distance constraints.
13. Create three lines connecting the centerpoint of the circle and the corner points, as shown.
14. Click the **Constrain equal** icon on the **Sketcher constraints** toolbar. Next, select two lines to make them equal in length. Select the third and second lines to make them equal.

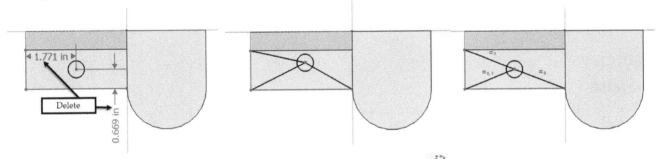

15. Select all the three lines and click the **Toggle construction geometry** icon on the **Sketcher geometries** toolbar.
16. Click **Close** on the **Combo View** panel.

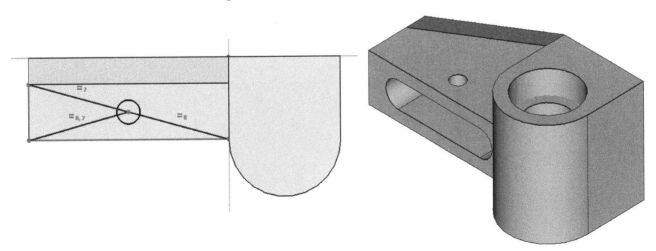

17. Now, change the size of the rectangular pad feature. Notice that the slot and hole are adjusted automatically.

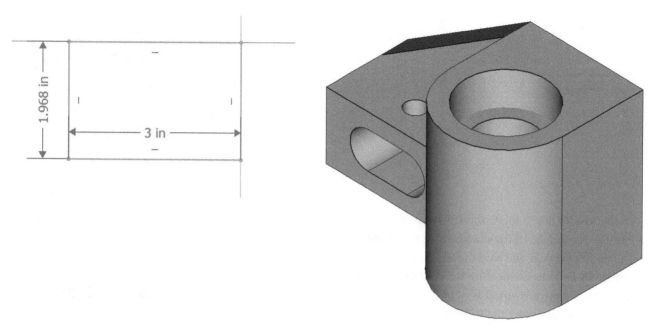

18. Save and close the file.

Exercises

Exercise 1

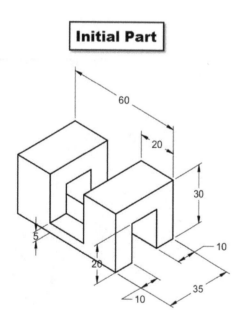

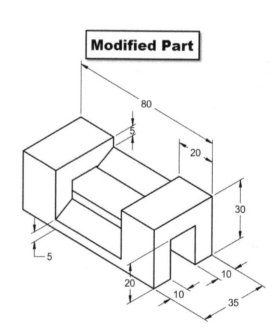

Exercise 2

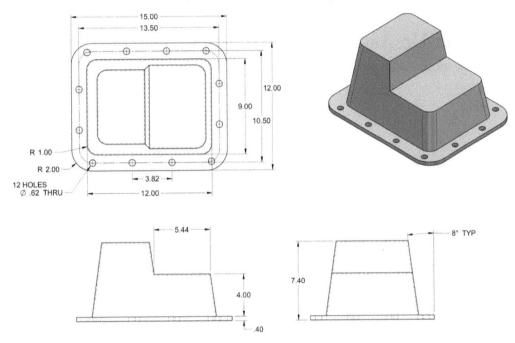

SHEET THICKNESS = 0.079 in

Chapter 9: Assemblies

Tutorial 1 (Bottom-Up Assembly)

In this example, you create the assembly shown below.

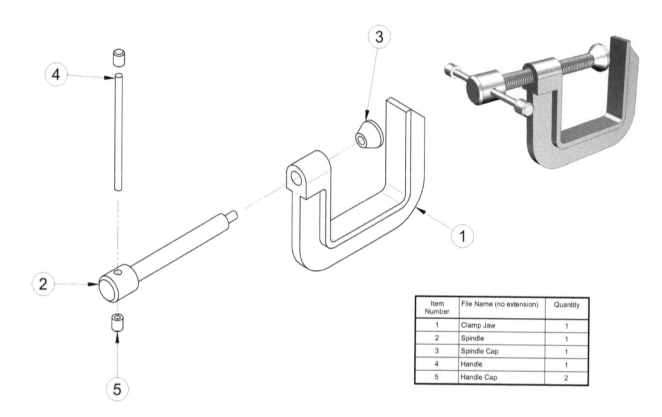

Item Number	File Name (no extension)	Quantity
1	Clamp Jaw	1
2	Spindle	1
3	Spindle Cap	1
4	Handle	1
5	Handle Cap	2

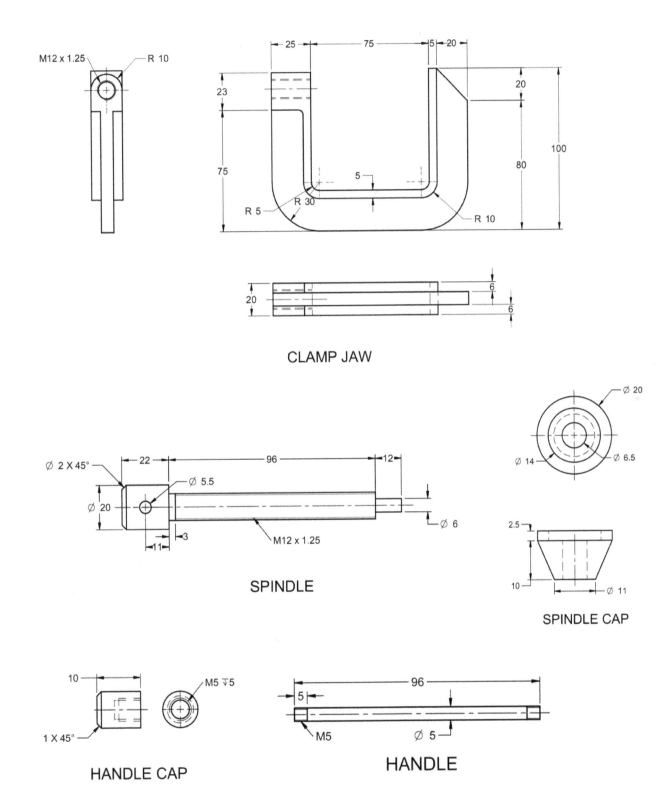

CLAMP JAW

SPINDLE

SPINDLE CAP

HANDLE CAP

HANDLE

Creating the Assembly file

1. Create the parts of the assembly. You can also get the part files by sending us an email to _freecadtuts@gmail.com_
2. Save all the part files in a single folder.

3. Click the **FreeCAD 0.18** icon on your Desktop to start FreeCAD.
4. On the **Start** page, click **Documents > Create New**; it creates a new document.
5. On the Menu bar, click **Tools > Addon manager**; the **FreeCAD** message box appears showing that the addons are not part of FreeCAD. Click **OK** to display the **Addon Manager** dialog.
6. Click the **Workbenches** tab and select the **A2plus** addon. Next, click **Install/update**.
7. Click **Close**; the **Please restart FreeCAD for changes to take effect** message appears. Click **OK**.
8. Close the **FreeCAD** application window. Next, click the **FreeCAD 0.18** icon on the Desktop.

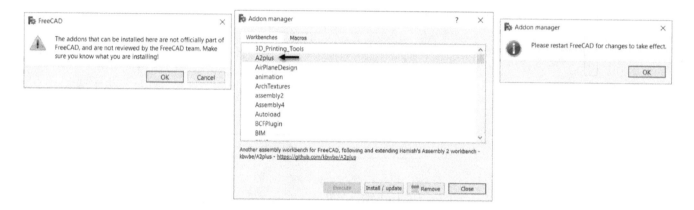

9. On the **Workbench** toolbar, select **Workbench** drop-down **> Part Design**.
10. Click **Edit > Preferences** on the **Menu** bar; the **Preferences** dialog appears on the screen.
11. Click **Units** tab and select **User system > Standard(mm/kg/s/degree)**.
12. Select **Number of decimals > 2** and click **OK** on the **Preferences** dialog.
13. Click **File > Save** on the Menu bar. Next, go to the location of the folder in which all the part files of the assembly are located. Enter **Tutorial 1** in the **File name** box and click **Save**.

Inserting part files in the Assemblies

1. Click the **Add a part from an external file** icon on the **A2p_Part** toolbar (or) click **A2plus > Add a part from an external file** on the menu bar; the **Select FreeCAD document to import part from** dialog appears.
2. On the **Select FreeCAD document to import part from** dialog, go to the folder in which all the part files of the assembly are located.
3. Select the **Clamp Jaw.FCStd** part file from the list, and then click **Open**; the clamp jaw is placed in the graphics window.
4. Click the **Add a part from an external file** icon on the **A2p_Part** toolbar (or) click **A2plus > Add a part from an external file** on the menu bar.
5. On the **Select FreeCAD document to import part from** dialog, click **Spindle.FCStd**, and then click **Open**. Click in the graphics window to place the component.

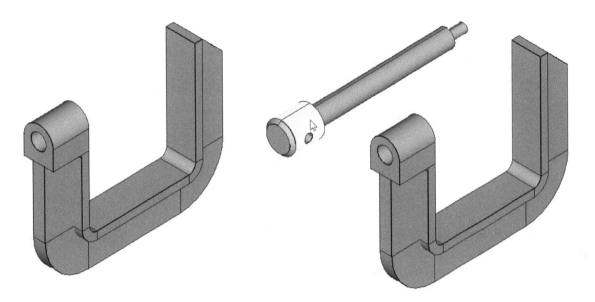

6. Likewise, insert the *Spindle Cap, Handle,* and two instances of *Handle Caps.* Next, click the green check on the **Insert parts and assemblies** dialog.

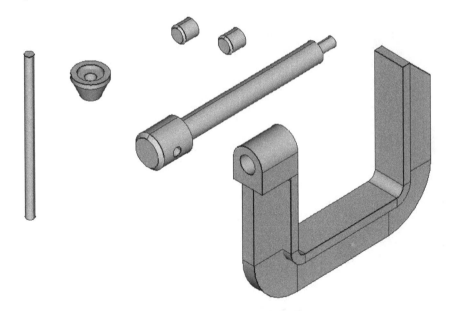

Defining Constraints

1. Press and hold the Ctrl key and select the flat face of the *Clamp Jaw,* as shown in the figure.
2. Rotate the model view and select the flat face of the model, as shown.
3. Click the **Add planeCoincident constraint** icon on the **A2p_Constraints** toolbar (or) click **A2plus > Constraint > Add planeCoincident constraint** on the menu bar.
4. On the **Constraint Properties** dialog, select **Direction > opposed**. Next, type 31 in the **Offset** box, and then click **Flip sign**. Click **Accept** to create the planeCoincident constraint.

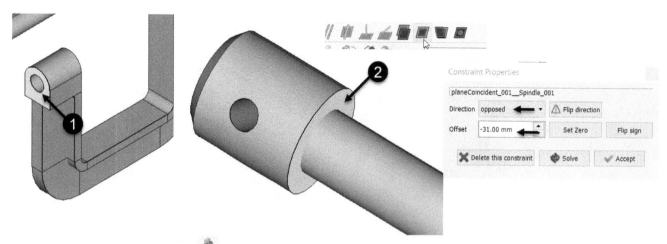

5. Click the **Define constraints** icon on the **A2p_Constraint** toolbar (or) click **A2plus > Constraint > Define constraints** on the menu bar.

6. Press and hold the Ctrl key and select the cylindrical face of the *Spindle* and hole of the *Clamp Jaw*.

7. Click the **Add axis Coincident constraint** icon on the **Constraint Tools** dialog.

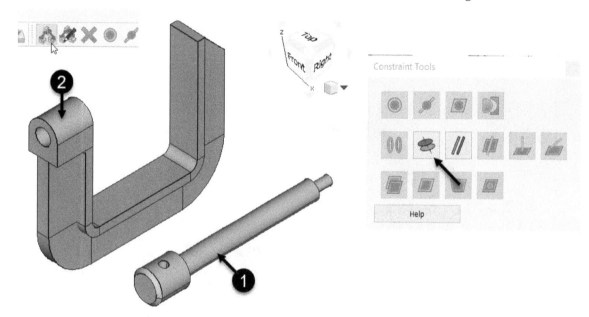

8. On the **Constraint Properties** dialog, select **Direction > aligned**. Next, select **Lock Rotation > True**. Click **Accept**.

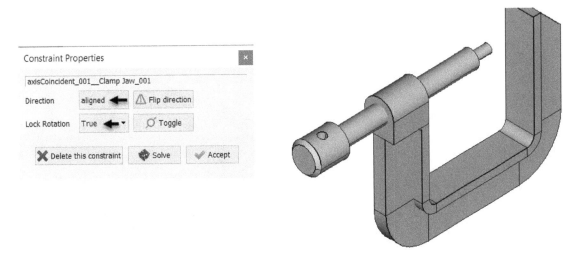

9. On the **Place Constraint** dialog, click **Type > Mate**, and then type **31** in the **Offset Value** box.
10. Click on the circular edge of the *Spindle Cap* hole, as shown.
11. Press and hold the Ctrl key and click on the circular edge of the *Spindle*, as shown.
12. Click the **Add circularEdge constraint** icon on the **Constraint Tools** dialog.
13. Select **Direction > opposed** on the **Constraint Properties** dialog; the *Spindle* and *Spindle Cap* are axially aligned and positioned opposite to each other.

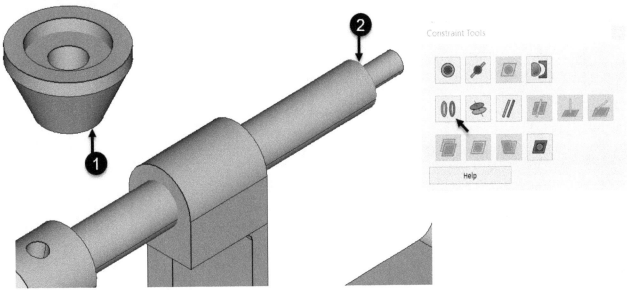

14. Select **Lock Rotation > True**, and then click **Accept**.

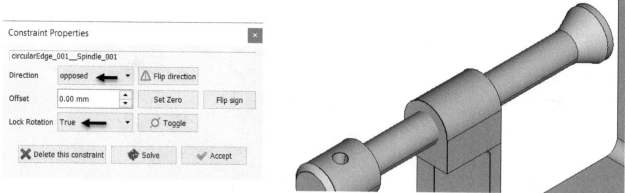

15. Press and hold the Ctrl key and select the cylindrical face of the *Handle* and the hole located on the *Spindle*.

16. Click the **Add axis Coincident constraint** icon on the **Constraint Tools** dialog.

17. Select **Lock Rotation > True**, and then click **Accept**.

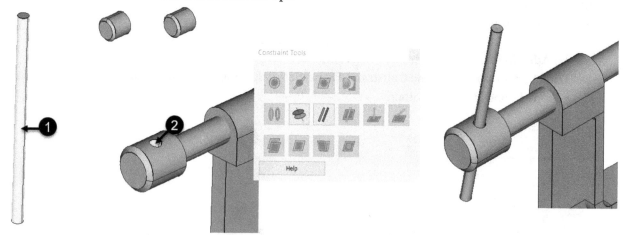

18. Press and hold the Ctrl key and click on the circular edge of the *Handle* hole, as shown.

19. Rotate the model and click on the inner circular edge of the *Handle cap*, as shown.

20. Click the **Add circularEdge constraint** icon on the **Constraint Tools** dialog.

21. Select **Direction > opposed** on the **Constraint Properties** dialog.

22. Select **Lock Rotation > True**, and then click **Accept**.

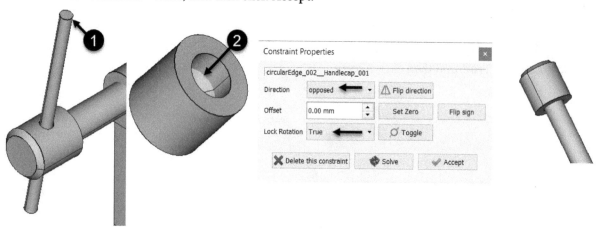

23. Press and hold the Ctrl key and click on the lower circular edge of the *Handle* hole, as shown.
24. Rotate the model and click on the inner circular edge of the second *Handle cap*, as shown.

25. Click the **Add circularEdge constraint** 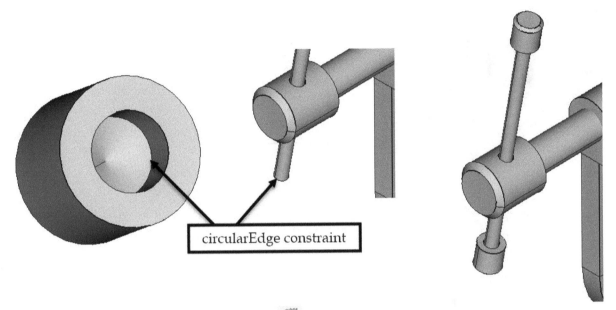 icon on the **Constraint Tools** dialog.
26. Select **Direction > aligned** on the **Constraint Properties** dialog.
27. Select **Lock Rotation > True**, and then click **Accept**.

circularEdge constraint

28. Click the **Print detailed DOF information** icon on the **A2p_View** toolbar (or) **click A2plus > View > Print detailed DOF information** on the menu bar; the degrees of freedom of all the parts are displayed.

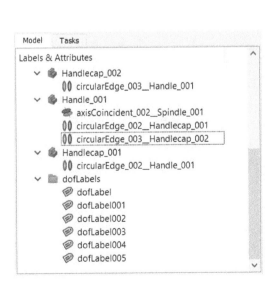

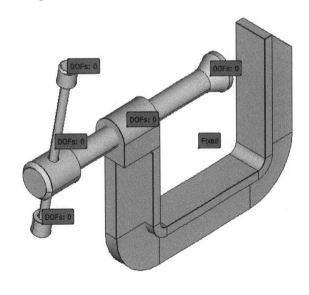

29. Click the **Print detailed DOF information** icon on the **A2p_View** toolbar to hide the DOF labels.
30. Save and close the assembly file.

Exercises

Exercise 1

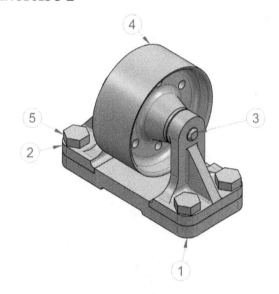

Item Number	File Name (no extension)	Quantity
1	Base	1
2	Bracket	2
3	Spindle	1
4	Roller-Bush assembly	1
5	Bolt	4

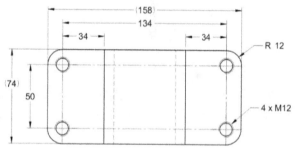

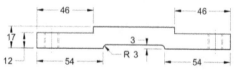

Base

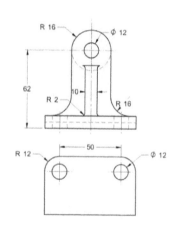

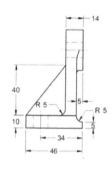

Bracket

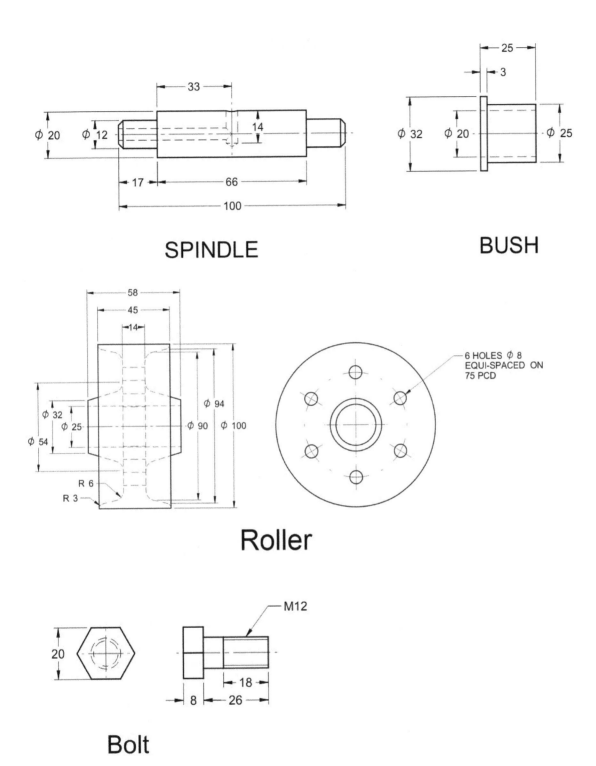

SPINDLE

BUSH

Roller

Bolt

Chapter 10: Drawings

Tutorial 1

In this example, you create the 2D drawing of the part shown below.

Creating a New Drawing

1. Download the **Chapter 10** part files from the companion website. Next, extract the zip file.
2. Click the FreeCAD icon on the Desktop.
3. Click **File > Open** on the Menu bar. Next, go to the location of the download files and double-click on the Tutorial1 file.
4. Select the **TechDraw** option from the **Workbench** drop-down (or) click **View > Workbench > TechDraw** on the menu bar.
5. Click **Edit > Preferences** on the menu bar. Next, select the **TechDraw** option from the left side of the **Preferences** dialog.
6. Click the browse button next **Hatch Image** box under the **Files** section. Next, go to the location C:\Program Files\FreeCAD 0.18\data\Mod\TechDraw\Patterns
7. Double-click on the **simple.svg** file.

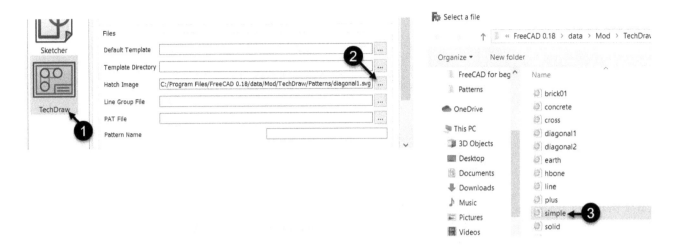

8. Select **Projection Angle > Third from the General** section.
9. Click the **TechDraw Dimensions** tab, and then select **Center Line Style > DashDot** from the **Decorations** section.
10. Click the **Center Line Color** swatch, and then select the Black color from the **Basic colors** section of the **Select Colors** dialog. Next, click **OK** twice.

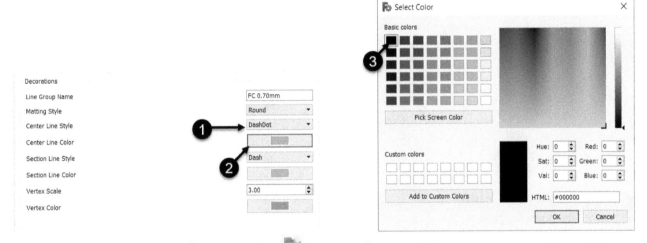

11. Click the **Insert new Page using Template** icon on the **TechDraw Pages** toolbar (or) click **TechDraw > Insert new Page using Template** on the menu bar.
12. Go to the location:
    C:\Program Files\FreeCAD 0.18\data\Mod\TechDraw\Templates
13. Select the **A3_LandscapeTD** template. Next, click **Open**.

Inserting the Base View
1. Click the **Tutorial 1** tab on the bottom of the window. Next, select the front face of the model.

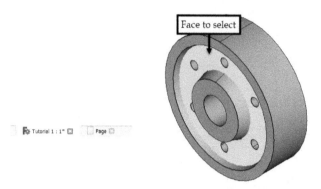

2. Click the **Page** tab on the bottom of the window.

3. To generate the base view, click the **Insert View in Page** icon on the **TechDraw Views** toolbar.

4. Click on the dotted borderline of the view. Next, press and hold the left mouse and drag the view to left.

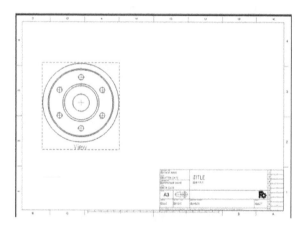

Generating the Section View

1. Select the base view.

2. Click the **Insert section view in drawing** icon on the **TechDraw Views** toolbar.

3. Click the **Looking left** icon on the **Quick Section Parameters** section.

4. Type **0** in the **X, Y,** and **Z** boxes, respectively. These values define the location of the section plane.

5. Type **A** in the **Symbol** box and click **OK** to create the section view.

6. Drag the section view and position it correctly. Make sure that it is horizontally in-line with the base view.

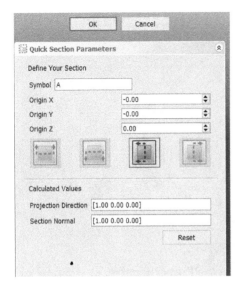

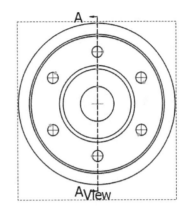

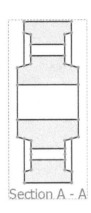

Inserting the Isometric View

1. In the **Combo View** panel, select the **Body** from the **Model** tab.
2. Click the **Insert View in Page** 🏛 icon on the **TechDraw Views** toolbar; the isometric view of the model is displayed on the drawing page.
3. Select the isometric view and click the **Data** tab on the **Property** panel.
4. Scroll to the **Base** section and change the **Scale** value to 0.5.
5. Click and drag the isometric view to the top-right corner.

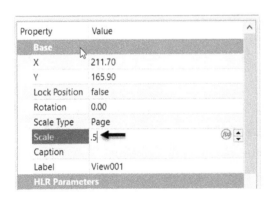

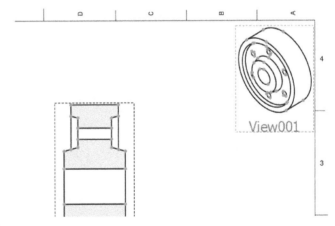

Adding the center lines to the drawing view

1. Select the base view from the drawing page. Next, click the **View** tab on the **Property** panel.
2. Scroll to the **Decoration** section and select **Horiz Center Line > true**.

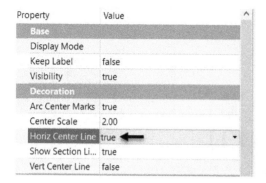

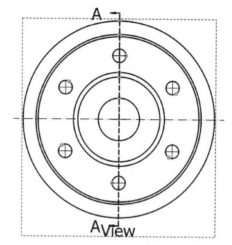

3. Select the section view from the drawing page. Next, click the **View** tab on the **Property** panel.
4. Scroll to the **Decoration** section and select **Horiz Center Line > true**.

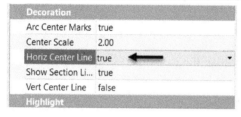

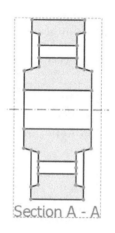

Adding Dimensions

Now, you add dimensions to the drawing.

1. Select the outer circular edge of the base view. Next, click the **Diameter dimension** icon on the **TechDraw Dimensions** toolbar (or) click **TechDraw > Insert a new diameter dimension** on the menu bar.
2. Click and drag the dimension outside the view.

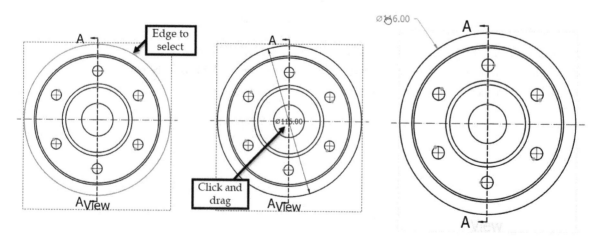

3. Likewise, add remaining dimensions to the base view, as shown.

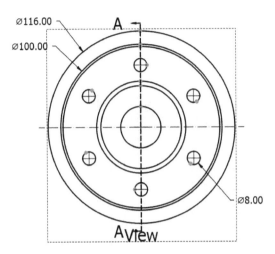

4. Select the diameter dimension of the small hole. Next, click the **Data** tab on the **Property** panel.
5. Click in the **Format Spec** box, as shown. Next, type **6 Holes** and press the SPACEBAR.
6. In the **Format Spec** box, click next to the diameter value and press the SPACEBAR.
7. Type **Equi-spaced on 75 PCD**. Next, click and drag the dimension.

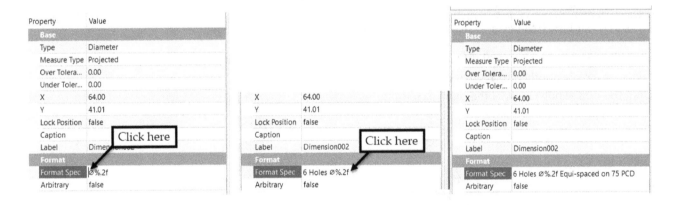

8. Press and hold the Ctrl key and select the vertices of the section view, as shown.

9. Click the **Insert a new horizontal dimension** icon on the **TechDraw Dimensions** toolbar.

10. Click and drag the dimension upward.

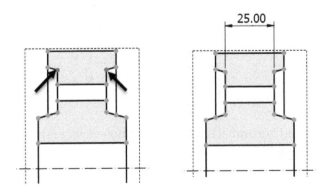

11. Press and hold the Ctrl key and select the vertices of the section view, as shown.
12. Click the **Insert a new horizontal dimension** ⊢⊣ icon on the **TechDraw Dimensions** toolbar.
13. Likewise, create another horizontal dimension.
14. Drag the dimensions upward, as shown.

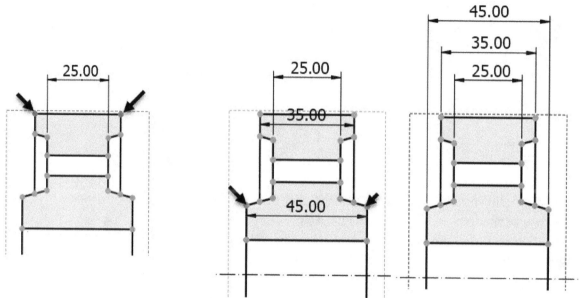

15. Press and hold the Ctrl key and select the two inclined lines in the detailed view, as shown.
16. Click the **Insert a new vertical dimension** ⊥ icon on the **TechDraw Dimensions** toolbar.
17. Likewise, create another horizontal dimension.
18. Drag the dimensions toward the right, as shown.

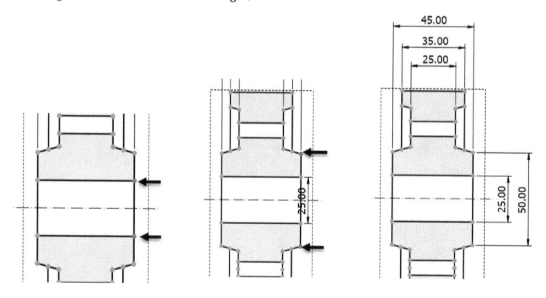

19. Press and hold the Ctrl key and select the inclined and horizontal edges of the section view, as shown.
20. Click the **Angle Dimension** icon on the **TechDraw Dimensions** toolbar.

21. Select the angular dimension value. Press and hold the left mouse button and drag the pointer toward left. Position the dimension, as shown.

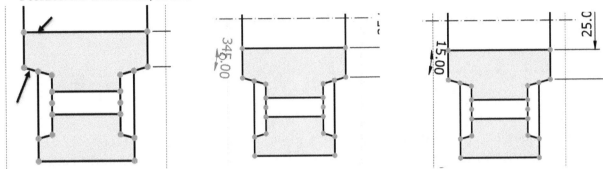

22. Select the angular dimension from the section view. Next, click the **Data** tab on the **Property** panel.

23. In the **Format Spec** box, click next to the dimension value and press the SPACEBAR. Next, type **TYP**.

24. Select any one of the diameter dimension from the base view. Next, click the **Data** tab on the **Property** panel

25. Select the diameter symbol from the **Format Spec** box. Next, right click and select **Copy**.

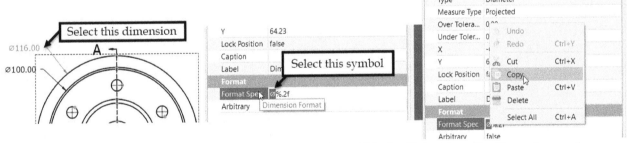

26. Select the vertical dimension from the section view. Next, click the **Data** tab on the **Property** panel

27. In the **Format Spec** box, click before dimension value. Next, right click and select **Paste**; the diameter symbol is pasted.

28. Click on the drawing sheet to update the dimension.

29. Likewise, add the diameter symbol to the vertical dimension with the value 50.

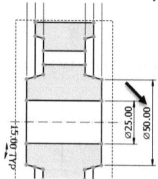

Populating the Title Block

1. Zoom in to the title block area. Next, double-click on the green square displayed on TITLE.

2. Type **Example 1** in the **Value** box, and then click **OK**.
3. Likewise, add data to the remaining fields in the Title block.
4. Save and close the file.

Exercises

Exercise 1

Create orthographic views of the part model shown below. Add dimensions and annotations to the drawing.

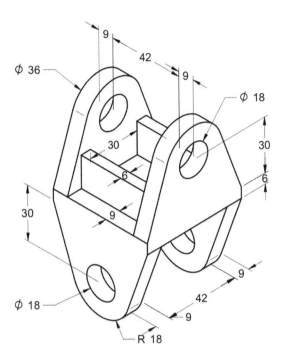

Exercise 2

Create orthographic views and an auxiliary view of the part model shown below. Add dimensions and annotations to the drawing.

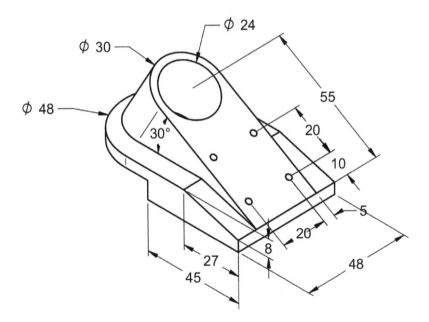